today and always
)but especially today(. III

xo. adrian michael

the words you needed to hear. here.
the words you needed to feel. here.
the words you needed to fill. here.
may you be showered. here.
may you be flooded. here.
may you be seen. here.
may this here
be everywhere
so you can always be
reminded of how necessary you are.
reminded of how beautiful you are.
reminded of how brilliant you are.
reminded of how deep you are.
you are special special treasure.
you already know this.

love hopes for you.

books by adrian michael

loamexpressions

blinking cursor

notes of a denver native son

blackmagic

lovehues

notes from a gentle man

blooming hearts

book of her book of she

for hearts that ache.

he was taught to be this way. I + II

giver. I + II + III

love hopes for you. I + II + III

xo. lvst.

words you didn't know you needed to hear.

love hopes for you. III

adrian michael

a lovasté project
in partnership with hwttbtw
published by
creative genius
CONCORDHAUS

lovaste.com

Copyright © 2021 by Adrian Michael Green

All rights reserved. No part of this book may be reproduced or transmitted in any form or by any means, electronic or mechanical, including photocopying, recording, or by any information storage and retrieval system, without written permission from the publisher.

Published by Creative Genius Publishing—
an imprint of lovasté

| Denver, CO | Concord, CA |

To contact the author:
    visit adrianmichaelgreen.com
To see more of the author's work:
    visit IG @adrianmichaelgreen
Book jacket designed by Adrian Michael Green

ISBN-13: 9798732313345

Printed in the United States of America

for lovers.
for those looking.
for those filling in
what others can't.

a playlist*

passport x masego
flotus x eric bellinger
i want you around x snoh aalegra
b.s. x jhené aiko + kehlani
lights out x h.i.m
countless times x marzz
stand for myself x yola
young & free x dermot kennedy
passing through x tobe nwigwe
you changed me x jamie foxx + chris brown
your everything x trevor jackson
under the moon x 070 shake
saving my love for you x kem
all to me x giveon
skipping stones x gallant + jhené aiko
is it any wonder? x durand jones & the indications
all i need x jacob collier + mahalia + ty dolla $ign
it was always you x maroon 5
para volar x camila meza
lessons x eric roberson
right x khruangbin
hold on me x esperanza spalding
3am x amaarae
free x 6lack
hope this makes you love me x tank
be good to me x jacob banks + seinabo sey

incense. palo santo. candles. sage.
tea. whiskey. wine. water. beer.

*to be listened to. lit and sipped while reading or between readings for ultimate experience.

*five agreements***

use to build trust and commitment. use to anchor you. use to focus you. use to remind you. use to find your way home.

be fully present. when you are doing this work be with this work. turn off distractions. when your attention goes away acknowledge its going and come back. come back.
lean into discomfort. if some concepts and language herein triggers you tells you close this go away from this stay this. stand in the fire a bit longer. this isn't an overnight read. let growth happen slowly.
host the journey. share this when it feels good to. with those close. with those you trust. to wonder together. to learn together. to push together. you not as expert. but you as light)one of the lights(to inspire healing magic to make better. to love better. to be better.
give you what you need. some of this may not land with you. some of this may not be a one-to-one. make it relevant to you. seek the lesson. translate it in ways that make sense to where you are in life.
honor your process. in moments of confidence and confidentiality you can keep you to you. keep this to you. never feel like you have to announce your story your journey your wondering. make sure that along the way you celebrate how far you have come.
practice. this isn't meant to just stay stagnant. this is meant to be breathed out and in. out and in. for yourself. for the world. to try out. to try on. to probe and fill holes and connect bridges and break down barriers. to deeper connect by seeing you in the mirror and the humanity of others you may not have seen before)really really seen(. so be willing to get messy. be raggedy. not perfect)never perfect(. to make room for you. to make room for others. you decide what this looks like feels like sounds like in practice. in real time. to learn and unlearn. learn and unlearn.

*to take with you on this journey. try them. scrap them. write your own. peace be unto you.
**copyright lovasté adpted by agreements encouraged by nais and the national equity project.

words for you

the most beautiful random message.	1
what people want.	2
insecurity is a love hope.	3
what you don't want to hear.	4
stop killing the ones you fear.	5
five you never know's.	6
five loving how's to begin checking in.	7
learning to let go of fear.	8
how is your heart is a love hope.	9
six perspective shifts.	10
seven golden rules.	11
two courageous acts.	12
i see you is a love hope.	13
six hammers and one nail.	14
you are already a great soul.	15
flattery.	16
three things out of your control.	17
continue being someone everyone needs more of.	18
four statements to say out loud.	19
there is a fear in you that doesn't belong to you.	20
five daily checkpoints to check.	21
you've changed is a love hope.	22
the many thanks you deserve.	23
highly highly.	24
break in peace.	25
listen. listen.	26
you're not for everyone.	27
if it doesn't meet your needs return to sender.	28
five could be doing's you don't have to be doing.	29
fill better.	30
when you find yourself being you.	31

words for you

a reminder that you're human.	32
five deep deep breaths.	33
five notes to write. read. breathe. repeat.	34
the greatest bet is the one you take on yourself.	35
a quick note on worry.	36
let your journey be yours.	37
longing for you.	38
little big things.	39
new season fresh.	40
thoughts on showing up for your person.	41
all about trust.	42
blossom into your next best version.	43
four signs you are done done.	44
missing you means more than i love you.	45
to remind you when they forget.	46
ready. ready. ready.	47
everything about you is a love hope.	48
stay close to people that make you feel seen.	49
control doesn't look good on anyone.	50
hope this one lands for you.	51
let the past be past.	52
moving slow is still moving.	53
read this one slowly.	54
the deep breath you been waiting for.	55
four do's they won't do for you.	56
the most beautiful where have you been.	57
ten treats to bring you joy.	58
they all hope it's you.	59
the kind of unforgettable memory that lasts.	60
an anti-hate statement.	61
look inward.	62

words for you

love lessons.	63
twelve you should be's.	64
possible possibilities.	65
the five protections.	66
you can't hear anyone that doesn't speak in love.	67
for when you need this.	68
another reminder to rest.	69
dear people who paused in june.	70
two types of trying to be done trying.	71
the worst kind of person.	72
a checklist. a heartlist.	73
if they want easy that isn't you.	74
nine types of love you deserve.	75
seven ways to eliminate self-doubt.	76
the greatest imprint.	77
you are loved.	78
twelve ways to push yourself through hard times.	79
where you'll find love.	80
you are a beautiful love.	81
let go of souls who just don't care.	82
only full love for you love.	83
thank you for getting you to you.	84
you're one of a kind. II.	85
the seven detachments.	86
six beautiful reminders for reminders.	87
you at half is still full.	88
you are more.	89
this part is meant to turn you into gold.	90
six pillow talk questions.	91
happiness is homemade.	92
selfish of you.	93

words for you

you shouldn't have to.	94
where to go.	95
your vulnerability makes you beautiful.	96
now is the time.	97
four realizations.	98
they can't tell your story.	99
what you are.	100
dodging heartache.	101
the kind of people to fall in love with. II.	102
the kind of person you already are.	103
get away from unaccountable people.	104
if they leave while you change. II.	105
once in a lifetime love.	106
twelve reasons.	107
thirteen things to always remember.	108
grow through what you are going through.	109
possibilities to let in.	110
what you deserve to feel.	111
pay close attention.	112
handle you with care.	113
what to focus on.	114
belonging is a love hope.	115
no one like you.	116
on leaving.	117
for when you just want to turn back.	118
four reminders to inhale twice.	119
never never too much too much.	120
twelve pressures to let go of.	121
four things we all have in common.	122
this one is to remind you to smile.	123
12 love lessons.	124

words for you

the ones for you.	125
you don't need.	126
what you need to hear but haven't heard.	127
love hopes for you.	128
love hopes for you. II.	129
love hopes for you. III.	130
truths about you.	131
your love hope is you.	132
how to)re(discover love.	133
you are the best love anyone could ever get.	134
how to)re(discover love. II.	135
you always love again.	136
necessary reminders.	137
what abundance finds.	138
healing words.	139
waves of you.	140
five ways to maintain meaningful connection.	141
what intimacy looks like.	142
thank you.	143
because of you.	144
because of you. II.	145
consistency you deserve.	146
if anything you are yours. always yours.	147
turn your sails towards yourself and keep sailing.	148
you get to decide.	149
when they want to come back.	150
if no one has told you yet.	151
i statements you deserve to feel.	152
your love is.	153
what doesn't exist.	154
love hopes that fill you.	155

the most beautiful random message
to say or send to someone you love.

you're my favorite favorite. favorite being.
favorite memory. favorite song. favorite
pastime. thinking of you now boosts
my mood and i thank you for your presence
in my life. what a present you are. i don't
say this enough. too many times)more than
i care to admit(i have failed to tell you.
i remember all the things you have enriched
in me. for me. just by being you. you must
have a super power because when i am off or
down you seem to know when to check-in.
when to add water to my soil. to my soft spots
i tend to forget about. i love you. i honor you.
i appreciate you. you are my my. my. my. my.

and you don't hear this enough or know this enough so i'm telling you. every my i can think of you are. every my i can think of you are. the greatest aria. the waves of you fill the holes in me. in every one. in every being. not even sure if this touches you in the ways you to deserve to face you in all the glory i need these words to but this is one of many many many many countless times i will carry the tides to your shore. to your feet. to your heart. and honor you. all you do. all you are. can't say it any differently. i can't. but i will try. this is my try. because my. my. my. so great you are. so grateful for you. a beautiful wonder to behold. if this strikes you to the core just imagine just imagine just imagine what it is you do for others besides you. beside you i will always be. thank you for being a living hope to breathe in. thankfull. forever my favorite being to be with.

how to fill more of this. turn to this over and over and over. as gesture as constant break to flip through the beautiful pages of you.

what people want.

consistency.
loyalty.
connection.
love.

what you want.

the same. and more. yet at times it feels at odds.
some would rather shatter all hearts and cause
trauma just so they can hoard and play keep away
as if there isn't a lot of life to share.
a lot of good to go around. they don't
know it)yet(but their own hurting
won't stop your joy. your living.
you are unstoppable.

so much heaviness happening. in you. around you. towards you. towards others. and as you try to make sense things just keep crumbling with no timeout. no timeaway. no break time just keeps ticking. ticking. repeating itself. wounded creating more wounds. harmed creating more harm. and there you are amidst the wreckage. noticing. wondering. wandering. curious and feeling many things at once because what was solid is no longer core. trying to find balance is your new challenge. but as you take it on remember your why. one of them. all of them. and no matter what comes at you you always find your way. nothing can ever stop a phoenix rising.

how to rise like a phoenix with your why. think about what motivates you. what drives you. what inspires you. write this down and remember.

insecurity is a love hope.
it says:

i am fearful that you will see a part of me
that makes me feel small. makes me feel
unattractive. i'm learning to accept my
blemishes as blessings. it takes more work
to hide than it does to live in full light. so
if i show you me promise to be gentle when
i am self conscious. self sabotaging. self neglecting.
hold my hand like i hold yours. remember
this is a process. i am a process. in process.
of becoming. and that takes wild courage.
forgive me if you think i am pushing or
fishing for validation. just know that each time
you share)in your beautiful way(that you see
me helps me stay firm. love me. all of me.

***

what people say about you carries weight. sometimes too much weight. some of us have the ability to brush it off like it weighs nothing. others of us the weight of words weigh heavy of judgment it latches and won't come off. you move around and navigate the world in ways that you didn't move before simply because of what is holding you back. uncovering those and overcoming those insecurities are liberating. a liberating process. especially when you let love in like light to weed out what has been keeping you hostage.

how to brush it off like it weighs nothing. don't take it personal. let their words fall off of you like water falls and keeps falling. but instead of letting it pool and build up let the water return to them. what they say and do has nothing to do with you. try this on more.

what you don't want to hear
but really really need to know.

america is sick. has been sick. because hate is a sickness. an illness. it terrifies the ones who clutch to it so tight because without it they don't know what to do. don't know what to replace it with. hate is an invisible comfort. a power tool. removing any aspect of it would show so much fear. fear of losing. fear of knowing. fear of seeing who they truly are)who they have always been(scared insecure embarrassed sad intimidated ashamed guilty souls. so the cloak stays on. the shadow stays shadow and deep hatred gets the light. they do not see they are the root of the problem because that's like asking water what water is. hate can't see itself.

you'd be in a constant rage too
if you could never heal from
everyday traumas.

it is all around. and you can sense it. you can feel it. and sometimes you can feel stuck not knowing what to say or do when is the right time to joke about something or if it's a subject to never mention. but you know there is this toxin that can't be avoided. people hating people for whatever reason. maybe because they make them uncomfortable. maybe because it goes against a value that was discussed)or not discussed(in your household or place of residence that was unwelcome and unkind. maybe the difference is too vast that anything out of your norm isn't default and what isn't default is weird and unbecoming and unacceptable and should be elsewhere instead around you.

how to be an ally. choose empathy and take a breath. wonder in that space instead of dismissing its existence. it will take time but try on being willing. be willing.

stop killing the ones you fear.

nothing that anyone hasn't already said will change the hearts of those with deep seated deep seeded deep conscious and unconscious hate. you can show a video of a public lynching they can be at the public lynching they can stare in the face of someone as they take their last breath and keep their hands in their pocket and still not understand. if this country really cared about its citizens we would be in a state of national emergency. we are in a state of emergency. but because hate can't see itself there is no big deal. only casting blame back like a kid who doesn't want to tell the truth about stealing a candy car. they don't see themselves as terrorists just misguided or has a history of mental illness that gives them benefit of doubt and should be walked out peacefully even after just gunning down other souls. no no no no hate can never let go of its rule because it must confess its wrongs its sins its power and be denied and judged and that just can't happen so hate makes lives harder and harsher. you don't want to hear this. you won't even read this. you will justify what the slain black person must have done to justify running him off the road. you don't want to hear this. all law enforcement has to say is that they feared for their lives and like candyland or monopoly they get out of jail free cards. you don't care because it isn't happening to you. admit it. but if it was your child your cause your culture you'd spend all the money close all the things until shit got figured out and make sure it never happened again. but back to back to back to back to back to back to back that goes back to chattel slavery just isn't enough. stop killing the ones you fear because what you have was never yours in the first place.

how to breathe this message in. with grace. with understanding. with tapping into those moments you felt rage you felt fear you felt anger you felt sadness you felt a part of you had gone missing. and then you tell yourself it's about the system and not you. ask yourself how do you defeat a system. from the inside. the work starts there.

five you never know's
to always keep in heart.

you never know what people are going through.
you never know who needs a helping hand.
you never know why someone leans on you.
you never know how hard someone is working.
you never know what you don't know.

but you care. always care. always kind. always
lead with good. when you open with no desire
or motive to get back those who stumble upon
you will remember how you treated them. with love.
for love is the great equalizer that no
amount of money can buy. stay giving. stay
aware. your positivity is a light that guides
people home and you never know it.

you never know the hurt someone is hurting.

there is that heart of yours. that gold of yours. that sensitive of yours. that feels and feels and feels and feels. and those around you just don't get it. they downplay it. misunderstand it. and you cry uncried tears because you think you need to be strong. need to contain. need to hold the well full. but the inspiration of you the light of you the lover in you is allowed to stop holding your breath and breathe. it's okay to admit you're not okay and hurricane for a bit. you do so much it's okay to sigh and sad and decompress that chamber you keep tight. unwind and remind yourself that warriors need rest, too.

how to rest. whatever you haven't been able to do. do that. repeatedly. joyously. unapologetically. seriously. candidly.

five loving how's to begin
checking in with someone.

how is it being you.
how may i hold you.
how has your heart been.
how might i support you.
how deep is your love today.

***

a lot is happening in you. around you. and while
you figure it out there can be pressure)too much
too much(to do a lot and be a lot for others. but
when you stumble upon lovers like you there is
sincere awareness of all of all of all of all the
hardship you sift through. and they want nothing
but for you to give them some of that to carry.

feeling burdensome is easy to keep you from retreating into people
and instead you choose to retreat into you. to be all things for you.
so not to overextend or put out anyone from their priorities. but
you are a priority. and it is okay to turn to someone and express
your needs. express your reservations. express your hesitation. you
would be surprised when the response you think you would get
actually is the waiting someone has been waiting for. so they can
extend a gasp finally to say finally i thought you'd never ask.

how to not feel like a burden. know that you aren't a burden. know
that you are a blessing. know that you deserve all the time you've
reserved and kept to yourself for someone to do the honors and
love on you for a change. for a chance to roll down your walls even
if briefly to feel unconditional love and kindess in your lungs.

learning to let go of fear.

instead of envious be encouraging.
instead of pretending be honest.
instead of in your head be out loud.

***

it is when you let go you realize what you've been blocking yourself from. it is when you let go you realize what you've been blocking others from. when you see someone you love hurting you help them. but you too have been hurting you've just gotten used to the pain. dedicate today and all the days you are granted that follow to heal you. to be honest with you. to breathe since you've been holding your breath. to be you and only you. and then you can see more clearly. love more clearly. love more deeply.

how to let go. notice when you get triggered by something. if your mood changes or you have an adverse reaction. probe into that in the interest of knowing something is there. deeper there. still there. festering but at a level causing some causes that you thought no longer caused you to care)or not care(.

how to let go of fear. notice what you are avoiding. what you are quick to say no to or what you are quick to remove from. many things you block yourself from are to protect you. there are some things you block yourself from that you know are keeping you from your true self. your true path. your true view. to know that just ask yourself: is this fear to protect me or is this fear to prevent me. your answers will tell you what you need to know.

how is your heart is a love hope.
it says:

don't think. just feel. breathe down down
and dive below the surface of your mind
where it has no jurisdiction. say what is
true. dig and pull and sift and wonder.
there is no right or wrong just love.
just you and you. don't hide from
you. not anymore. take as much
time as you need. i'm not here
to judge. i'm here to love you.

***

whether it is you that is checking in on you or someone who loves you checks in on you don't give the automatic i'm fine or i'm good. tell the truth. no need to sugar coat if you're feeling salty or sour or spoiled or sad. give it straight no preamble. no preface. then you can spend more time being real and less time holding your breath. you can spend more time being genuine and unmasked and less time ingenuine and masked. your heart is a special beacon a special messenger a special rendering. so to deny the true sound of it the true pound of it the true might of it changes the beat of it the raw of it the feel of you. be true to you.

how to speak the language of your heart. mark the initial response when asked how you are doing. be conscious that is to recognize if you maneuver away or towards that honesty. towards that reality. and if you pull back just be interested in why. try to say the first thing more. try not to limit your heart based off what you think they want to hear. ask yourself: what isn't being said here. say that.

six perspective shifts.

life is too short so tell people you love them.
never say you don't have time because you do.
be honest and say your time is being used elsewhere.
fifteen minutes of joy is better than no minutes of joy.
schedule time for you to refill.
figure out what you want and what kind of person you want before committing so you can communicate what a healthy relationship looks like and feels like for you and vice versa.

***

there are so many sides to a story to a situation to an event. so what you see and experience will be different from the person you may have been a witness too. it isn't worth blaming or shaming or guilting anyone from not saming or seeing or duplicating your interaction to justify your behavior or your feeling. yours is yours. theirs is theirs. if there is similarity then cool. if there isn't similarity then cool. the price you keep paying from the energy you exhaust proving or disproving something is energy better suited just being. there is no hierarchy of experience there is only experience. the happening. the happened. the happen. so be in the moment and be open to perspective shifts.

how to see other sides. resist the urge of being defensive. listen calmly. wait for them to finish. don't listen to respond. listen to understand. listen to empathize. listen to wonder. before making a judgment allow judgment to cross your mind without verbalizing it out loud. judgments are normal. perspective is yours to sit with and be curious if there is more. there is always more.

seven golden rules.

you can't plan everything but even an intention is a plan that needs action. people who are unhappy can still be your biggest advocates. a fool is someone who judges other people and gets upset when others pass judgment on them. a closed heart is closed for a reason. don't expect others to support you when you don't support anyone or anything. you can't rush through life to get to a fairy tale ending you'll miss the point of your journey)spoiler: the rushing is your ending(. and if what you have doesn't feel like enough make it enough until your wings outgrow.

how to act. move even if you don't know where you're going.

how to honor your advocates. thank them every chance you get.

how not to be a fool. don't be foolish by misjudging others.

how to respect a closed heart. don't try to force it open.

how to gain support. support others without expecting it in return.

how not to rush. wonder why you want to rush then slow down.

how to make something enough. cherish what you have.

two courageous acts.

the courage to be yourself.
the courage to allow others
to do the same.

***

a lot of loss is happening. daily. hourly. moment to moment. and we're all just bracing ourselves for the next and the next and the next and the next. this doesn't feel real. feels unanything anyone has a guidebook to explain and help us navigate through.

so maybe just remember this. love deeply. love boldly. don't hold back because you may not hold again. live loudly. exist boldly. make each person you meet feel like they're the only only in the room. and when someone you know is gone or someone you know's someone is gone hold them. in your thoughts. in your mantras. in your steps. to continue. to keep their memory alive. to always recall. to never forget. to never forget.

i see you is a love hope.
it says:

i appreciate you. i honor you. and more than that
you need to deeply know that every ounce of me
thinks of you when you think i'm not thinking of
you. every little thing you do makes a huge ripple
makes the corner of the world i exist in brighter.
more significant. more bearable. and sometimes
)a lot of too many times(you feel unseen. under
looked. dispensable. unimportant. and that hurts
me to know you feel like that. the small things from
you are monumental. all that you do is admirable.
your effort is palpable. your heart is unlike any other.
and when you are down and look around
i hope you sense me. sending you all the love. all
the words no one has told you. i am proud of you.

this message is for me. this message is for you. this message is for all of us who find ourselves lifting. heavy things. light things. crating emotions and boxing away to-do's to get to later because right now isn't the best time. because right now is a hard time. because right now is a dark time. this message is for me. this message is for you. this message is for all of us who find ourselves giving. breathing deep breaths but not much breath is coming back. for those grinding with no oil. for those longing unrequited. for those wishing into an abyss that feels bottomless. this message is coded for those who can decode it the way it was meant to be received. if it doesn't hit you now it will hit you later. so save this and come back to it. to be seen is being loved and understood without words. i see you. i see you. i see. you.

how to see someone. look where you haven't looked before.

six hammers and one nail.

you can rush or you can patient.
what comes too fast may not last.
what comes slow is worth the wait.
your process is your process. no one
can speed up your bloom. only you
can grow at your own pace. all this
to say that you can so badly want
to skip and pass up the journey
to get to the other side and
to have the glory but not
working for it makes it
meaningless.

***

no one can speed up your bloom. the journey is what brings you joy. whatever happens after that is just an end of an epic adventure. and the entering into another occasion. the entering into a new.

how to appreciate the journey. slowly inhale the presence of the present. do not zoom through a moment. take in the moment by honing in your breath to the same pace as to what is around you and divide that by everything. freeze it in your body stillness. shutter your eyes like the shutter of a camera. keep them shut for a minute to remember what you just took in. this note will be one of many but the small of smallest detail will jolt your memory to that moment right before you closed. if you do this at least once when you find yourself trying to speed through you'll even catch a lesson.

you are already a great soul.

you are already a great soul.

***

give it your best. give it your all. give everything.
no matter if it is low stakes or high stakes you are
your own teacher. your own lesson. your body
keeps score. your mind takes notes. your heart
remembers the details. if it doesn't work out you
can say you did your best. tried and poured and
showed up the way you would want to be showed
up for. so whatever direction things go hold your
head up like the sun. bold and steady and radiant.
the goal is never to be perfect. the goal is to feel
you did everything you possibly could to help.
to love. to care. to be.

how to avoid perfectionism. celebrate the raggedy and the jaggedy the messy and the faily things you failed at but you tried at. pass on those bigger victories to show their summit isn't as grand as the smallest hill you climbed. for the first step is as grand if not grander than the one you look last. it may recalibrate what you place significance on. noting each grain of sand is still sand. it is the collective mound that should be applauded.

how to be a great soul. care. and keep caring. no matter the matter. no matter what isn't given in return. no matter what is out of your control. let nobody determine the gear you show up in. never. never.

flattery.

if you imitate you
then that)and that only(
is the sincerest form
of flattery.

emulate yourself. inspire yourself. be yourself.
make sure you love yourself enough to find out who you are.

***

you compliment you.
you validate you.
you see you.
you love you.
you appreciate you.

you being you is the mission. the inspiration.
never take yourself out of your own equation.

how to be you. how to flatter you. you daily. that's it. daily you. choose you. select you to priority and you to honor. not as trophy but as muse. to decide that what you are and who you are is and that is worthy of all the worries to know you don't have to question your worth again. so put you on. encourage you when all you want to do is doubt you. count on you. to respond how you need to respond and don't discount you. gas you. take all the fuel you light others with and become all the fireworks and magic firestorms that follow. that light up you is the light this world can no longer deny.

three things out of your control.

what people think of you.
how people talk about you.
when people fall for you.

you can't make anyone do anything they don't
want to do. you can't make anyone feel things
they don't feel. and that is why love from you
is the greatest love. you aren't forcing.
you are about loving. and anything with love
is always alluring. you are alluring.

***

don't forget what you focused on when you had time for yourself. do not go back into auto drive and re-prioritize things that pulled you away from you. center you. balance yourself back to yourself and do not sacrifice your wellbeing for a person who only cares about you clocking in. who only cares that you make their life comfortable. who only reaches out when they need something. do not forget your needs. this is the true test to see what you will do will that growth you been doing. all that unlearning you been doing. all them boundaries you been setting.

how to keep your momemtum. walk the walk. love yourself more. choose yourself more. look at the timeline of your unpacking and anchor you. goal set you. know that there is always something to do about you not in the polishing but in the giving. in the loving. in the grace you give yourself that you mostly give to others instead of you. can't keep sacrificing for someone if there is nothing of you left. so in your awareness check your energy and be your own meter.

continue being someone everyone needs more of.

it may take other people a lot longer to get you. to see you. to grasp your why. to understand the issues that keep you up at night. to care enough to shoulder some of what burdens you. to step out of their own shadow and recognize their light is what blinds others. the thing about life is that everyone isn't probing their own biases and their own traumas and their own sadness. they are carrying what was thrust upon them. that doesn't mean go back to sleep. it means continue being a mirror. continue being someone everyone needs more of.

***

not everyone will listen to your message or listen to your cries or listen to the rhythm of you. whether they care or not that doesn't mean shut yourself off. if one person is inspired to be less judgmental and more open and more loving because of you then you are to have saved a thousand lives. because that one person will inspire one person that will inspire another and another. my what a ripple you are. my what a ripple you make. don't let anyone dampen your heart. for that can't happen. you've already made this world better.

how to continue being someone everyone needs more of. trust in the solitude and the quiet of you. in the highs and lows of you. just by showing up and doing the smallest thing or saying the things you say make beautiful waves of change in the hearts and bodies and minds of others. speak out as you speak out even if others don't respond to it. someone was thinking it. you were thinking it. and soon they will do as you did and say what others couldn't at the time. resist the urge to be someone else. you are you for a reason.

four statements to say out loud.

say what you truly mean.
say what you truly feel.
say what you truly want.
say what you truly need.

toss away old patterns you've been watering that
were self limiting. that were compressing every
truth before the real you could come up for air.
say the first thing that comes to mind without
fear of losing anyone. if they are yours they
will accept you as you are. be yours
more often too.

***

when you are yours more often you thrive better when you surround yourself with people who get you. who love you. who see you. who want the best for you. those same people can cause you to limit you. to close you. to tell you what is best for you. if in your heart and in your soul you are being pushed away from your truth then i urge you to listen to yourself more. decide to re-decide where your roots are. sometimes you have to move away and find crisper air to remind your lungs what true breathing feels like. take good care of you and notice the impacts your words and behaviors have on others. you aren't exempt from being a limition to people either.

how not to limit others. give them space to be. to process their process. do not place judgment or lens their situation from your stage in life. ask more open ended questions. don't be a stone wall.

there is a fear in you that doesn't belong to you.

there is a fear in you that is keeping you.
there is a fear in you that is hostaging you.
there is a fear in you that is denying you.
there is a fear in you that is weighting you.
there is a fear in you that is draining you.
there is a fear in you that is stopping you.
there is a fear in you that is warning you.

so what will you do with it. when will you speak
to it. whose life are you living. what are you living
for. can you be happy with how things are love.
there is a fear in you that doesn't belong to you.

***

here it is again. a passage on fear. it doesn't go away as quickly as you would like it to. it creeps up when you least expect it to. it shows it's presence in ways that you may not recognize but if you were to probe and slow you'd see it. you'd see it. but now is your opportunity)there is always opportunity(to decode it. to size it. to pocket it. to shovel it. to cover it. to peace it. to welcome it. make it less about getting rid of it and more about having it take up less and less and less and less and less of your bandwith.

another how to on letting go of that fear in you. surprise it with your reaction or non reaction to it. fear is powered by your giving up to it and stopping what it is it wants stopping. when you speak counter to it you bring it with you even if your body is redding or your body is warming or your heart is throbbing or your heart is hearting or your mind is calculating or your mind is noing. there is a fear in you that no longer belongs. give it a timeline to move out.

five daily checkpoints to check.

listen more. pause more.
slow more. trust more.
love more.

don't hold yourself from
what others want for themselves
but don't want for you.

how to listen more. with every piece of you intently. quiet your mind by noticing when your stuff is keeping you from what they are sharing. then return to their voice. to listen to yourself do the same.

how to pause more. find moments of grace within each hour to start. take the last ten minutes before the next hour begins and stand up. walk. stretch. set your gaze away from what you are doing.

how to slow more. remind yourself there is no rush. even when you feel the pressure to fast to quick to zoom ahead. take a breath to slower your heart rate. apply this practice to every relationship.

how to trust more. think about what it might feel like for someone to wholeheartedly believe in you. what that would do for you. do that for them. do that for you. make a plan to fill that feeling.

how to love more. pay attention to the most miniscule thing about a person. keep a record of what they say how they say it why they say it. randomly and genuinely bring what you learned about the details of them in conversation in gift in service in honor of their life and shine their light back to them. this gesture of seeing them tells them you are attentive. that your attention is on every moment of them even when they don't think you are attending them.

you've changed is a love hope.
it says:

you're allowed to be who you are. to shift.
to become the someone you weren't ready
to become just yet. to become the sun just
as the sun has always been. to dune and
be strong and gather and be soft. time
hasn't always been good to you but
whatever you have been doing has
altered you in constant waves to
retrieve pieces as gentle notes
do. to remind you. and you
are someone to be proud
of. i honor your growth.

***

if someone expects you to be exactly who you used to be when they first met you let that expectation not barricade you into that one season of you. the people for you the community for you the someone for you will beside you always you celebrate you for being the being you are and breathe with the you you become and become and become again and again and again as if your reunion was the only thing they looked forward to like water awaits the sun to shadow on its surface. changing is what you do by choice and if they don't like it or they can't appreciate the good change you are then they don't really see you. they never really saw you when they first met you.

how to recognize change. you appreciate the in-between. the process it took to get where you are. in the appreciation you notice a difference when it arises. and then you ready yourself for the next change and the next change and the next.

the many thanks you deserve.

thank you for being. being there.
being available. being loving.
being rock. being water.
being magic. being understanding.
being you. being beautiful.

***

you deserve every thank you. every appreciation. every validation. every spotlight. every molecule in all the beings must pause and give you moments of accolade. because a heart like yours is made of the purest love. and pure love is like pure air. necessary and rare.

how to properly thank you. it isn't possible but it is in the trying. in the pursuit of giving flowers while giving flowers is possible. but a flower doesn't need another flower only light. so a proper thank you looks like not blocking the sun. looks like not damming your water. looks like not hurting your stem. looks like not clipping your petals. the best kind of thank you comes in the language that which is you.

highly highly.

your chapter is your chapter. it is easy to look at
other people and see what they have compared to
you. how much happiness how much stuff how
much more life and love you think they have.
but don't let the mirage of anyone else fool you
or tense you or influence the galaxy you create.
their chapter thirty won't ever be in your book.
you may have similar words but the energy is
what sets you apart. you are incomparable.
and it is the beautiful human in you that attracts.
that defines and makes language itself. all the stars
are you. your gravity is such sweet heart.

memorize the lines of you. not the lines of others
who just recycle the words from you.

***

be your favorite person's favorite person. because you are highly favored. highly loved. highly highly. don't get stuck on what others show you. be committed to the heart inside you and trust you'll get to what is meant for you.

how to focus on you. make an agreement with yourself to spend zero seconds comparing yourself with another. when you feel the gossip slip from your lips pull it back in. remind yourself they aren't you. remind you that yours is not theirs. and vice versa. speak kindly to their haves. water your haves. water your wants. water your needs. make plans to grow more of whatever you want to grow.

break in peace.

you don't have to always be profound. or present
yourself as perfect or take on the mantel as being
all knowing or figured out. there is room for you
)always room for you(to not know. to follow.
to give yourself grace to fumble and falter and
look to others for guidance. there is nothing wrong
or weak about asking for help. to be unsure. to commit
to life-long learning. to admit and take responsibility.
to not think that you have to always be strong. take a break.
break from standards. break from ego. break from
people you need to break from. break in peace.

how to break in peace. there are things called boundaries that many get weary about. as if it is your duty to tip-toe about your own space and your own needs. respectfully announce what has to happen for you to feel peace. and if they don't respect it this is your exit to turn.

how to break from ego. ask yourself if this is about being right or being heard. if it is about being right you are feeding your ego. step back and be courageous enough just to be heard and that be okay.

how to life-long learn. wonder what is more out there. what has changed. what is new. what is different. where are the gaps. what can be added. who haven't you heard from. who is missing from your perspective from your counter. be willing to unlearn.

how to give yourself grace. others will be harsh or critical in your day-to-day. be the one that is soft and gentle with words to yourself.

how to ask for help. say out loud that this may be difficult for you. that you've tried on your own but need guidance. your feelings are valid. take them with you in your seeking.

listen. listen.

the most heartbreaking tragedy is happening. loved ones aren't talking. aren't loving. aren't listening to the cries of each other. to the hopes that hopefully become reality before their eyes open one last time. it is important to have our own opinions. our own judgements. our own reasons. but not when they are barriers to the life of someone else. not when you shut your own family member out and away because you see in them what you've broken in you and envy their choice to be themselves and you hate them for it. banish them for it. to think one day we will wake up and every soul will be kind and welcoming isn't enough. act. do not wait for a cause to care. we are family. connected through life. do the right thing. care.

families are being divided. ripped apart. because people dig their heels in and choose to believe in things that are equitable and fair and just and good and kind. because people dig their heels in and choose to not believe in things that are equitable and fair and just and good and kind. it is as if empathy is broken or empathy is a practice only if the people look like and sound like and love like and believe like and earn like and vote like you. bridge better. listen better. love better. all that old information that has been given down to generation to generation that says we are the default and everyone else does our bidding is)and has always been(greedy and problematic. we need more compassion and more openness and more care. disagree? listen. biased? listen. don't know? ask and learn. no more us versus them. practice togetherness.

how to listen better. when your mind wants to force your mouth to let a response come out you stop the sound with a deep breath in and set your eyes and heart back on the person speaking on the person being vulnerable. not with the intent to rebuttal but with the intention to appreciate their story. then repeat back what you heard.

you're not for everyone.

you're not for everyone. you are for love.
you're not for everyone. you are for more.
you're not for everyone. you are for love.
you're not for everyone. you are for more.

it is not on your shoulders to play middleground.
to remain between trying not to offend or disrupt
or ruffle feathers. but the time to tread lightly is over.
the time is to be for something. for people.
for all beings. i hope you choose to be on the side
of love. more love. all love. deep love. real love.
that is what liberation is. when all of us are free.

***

you are the difference. the bridge. the fire starter. don't be fearful of standing on the side where you'd want others to be if parts of you were televised and brutalized and stereotyped and demonized and weaponized and criminalized and terrorized.

think seven generations ahead and understand the herstory you are making. do you want to leave this place better than you found it or do you want to maintain the backs of labor and division and the corruption and the horrible conditioning of people to continue.

be the change we all deserve to experience.

how to be for freedom. write down all the things you are able to do. write down all the things you personally do not want others to be able to do. if they can't do what you can do then be for their liberation not for their limitation. abolish your blindspots and bias.

if it doesn't meet your needs return to sender.

if it doesn't meet your needs return to sender.

five could be doing's you don't have to be doing.

you could be moving at a fast pace.
you could be in a one-sided relationship.
you could be changing yourself for others.
you could be giving away your time.
you could be thinking something in you is flawed.

as you are
is perfect.
as you are
is enough.
you are someone
the only one. like you.

***

more of you. all of you. full of you. you are someone. the only one. like you. i love that about you.

how to know you're enough. when people proclaim that you're too much. you know you're enough. relax your desire to want to respond and tell them about themselves. they may already know unkindness is within them. it isn't on you to teach them about them. it's on you to know you don't need to give them any energy.

fill better.

the lull that you are feeling is a message. the quiet.
the calm. the silence of just your thoughts. before
you go trying to fill it with noise. with distraction.
with substance. don't. pause and listen to the void.
that gap you think should be covered with action
with stuff with attention with someone is actually
your chance to fill it with you. to stop and wonder
what it is you really need. what you really crave.
what you really deserve. and where you went last
but didn't feel good after or during or even now
is a signal that you shouldn't go again. do again.
this window is your opportunity to get better.
fill better.

***

every day may not be a highlight or an excitement. it may feel empty or basic or drag with no purpose. but you are in it. in that part of your season that can feel alone or meaningless or thankless or stale. whatever you are feeling don't fill up on things and people that don't make you feel better. reading this you know what i mean. start now. start. now.

how to fill better. read this page again. and again. and again. then)only then(underline the next lines.

life isn't always going to feel good but you can control your thoughts and actions on how you decide to fill your life in with. when you fill there will be outcomes. ensure your intention is positive and let what pours out pour out.

when you find yourself being you.

sometimes you have nothing to say.
sometimes you have too much to say.
sometimes you have nothing to feel.
sometimes you have too much to feel.
sometimes you have nothing to do.
sometimes you have too much to do.

when you find yourself being you. being caught between extremes and become stuck or have to be overly apologetic. to come up with all the words all the reasons why you are how you are. don't do that. accept yourself. even if no one else will.

***

how to be you. overthink. overfeel. overwhatever. or vice versa. high and low. just notice this about you. understand this about you. learn this about you. accept this about you.

people will always have the capacity to say something about you. let them say it. you can't dictate their words. but you can sway your own words about your own being to be as you want them to be. as you want to be. become who you want to become by being okay with having nothing to say or too much to say or nothing to feel or too much to feel or nothing to do or too much to do. you are the measure. the decider. the factor. if you say it is then it is. being you is the dopest thing you will ever do for you when you do it the way you want to do it not how someone else prescribes it. love you on the road of self acceptance. all the other stuff will fall in love with you as you show up for you. be patient with you. this may take time.

a reminder that you're human.

right now)all at once(you are doing your best
to water familyships. friendships. partnerships.
situationships. workships. randomships. and
the heat keeps getting turrned up on you to juggle
and exceed and tend and provide and show up and
be present for all of it. for all of them. then there
is the relationship with yourself. the one that most
often gets the least attention. the tension is high.
on you trying to please everyone everyone. yet
you are the one left to fix it all. mend them all.
it's okay to prioritize and away message. to mute.
you are human. so human. give yourself grace.

***

how to prioritze you. take out that calendar you have. analog or electronic. go to this week. go to this day. and block out an hour. for a title call it me time. call it away time. call it break time. call it whatever it needs calling. and make sure you mark it as busy in case this is the type of calendar others can schedule meetings)pointless meetings(anytime they like. then do this for the next day. and the next. and the next. and the next. do this for all twelve months. as many blocks as you can. turn you into a habit. let your hour be your hour. fill it how you see fit. do something. do nothing. but let it be of your choosing. of your timing. of your willing. and make no apologies for it. do all that you can to make sure you do not do not do not reschedule you. you have done that enough)too many enoughs(and if people need that hour you can graciously say you are unavailable but if there are other times that work for them you'd be happy to accommodate. this is how you prioritize you.

five deep deep breaths.

you are almost there. reset. deep breath. take what you need with you and release what holds you back from love from light from healing from hope from gold from compassion from you.

***

i hope your heart is good. that it is in a rhythm of your choosing. of your desire. that you are safe and overflowing with love.

how to know if your heart is good. you know you. and sometimes your person knows you better than you know you. sometimes. but if they aren't there to tell you things like they notice you're a bit on edge than normal or that you're short with them more than usual that you're defensive when you typically aren't as defensive or that there is something they can't put their finger on but that something has got them catching your vibe a certain way you must be able to vibe that for yourself. gauge your emotions on the days you feel balanced and at peace and record all the words all the colors all the sounds you experience or would describe when balanced or at peace. this could be when you are doing things that bring you joy or are around the people that ignite you or working on the initiatives that energize you. keep doing this for all the things you do and look for a pattern. when are you high. when are you low. when you are in-between. do it especially when you find yourself catching moods that aren't necesarily moods for you. this kind of check in practice gives you the reins to see your own self. you'll know how your heart is by the heartbeats when you see the peaks when you see the values. you'll find a name for it. in whatever language you speak. the key then is to work on finding center in that hour of you.

five notes to write. read. breathe. repeat.

enough playing small. nothing small about you.
enough being taken for granted. you deserve more.
enough biting your tongue. let your words roar.
enough receiving empty love. refuse less than full.
enough going back to broken promises. peace them.

enough. enough. enough.

be the person that abandons wrong treatment. wrong ideas. wrong love. because that is what takes away inflated pride. some people need to be told about themselves. by your presence or by your absence.

***

how to let your absence speak. expectations to be where you are not appreciated can wear you out. you have been wore out to the point where you can think of one example too many. no need to make any announcement of you not being there. just don't there. do not rsvp. do not provide excuses. do not respond. this isn't about playing games it is about giving them information. for what it is like for what it will be like for what it should be like when you aren't around not because you can't be but because you won't be. won't be mistreated. won't be undervalued. won't be taken advantage of. call it a warning call it a yellow card call it what it is. notice how you feel in the gap of your absence. this may be what you need to declare in sabbatical you granted yourself which was long overdue.

the greatest bet is the one you take on yourself.

the greatest bet is the one you take on yourself.
there will be some who will always believe you
cannot change. there will be some who wait and
want to see you fail. there will be some who no
matter what they stay and stand in your corner.
so always remember to believe in you. to focus
less on the vocal doubters and hone in on your
inner value. your inner courage. your inner will.
your energy is priceless and your worth beyond
any number. you are where you are because of
the trust and faith and resilience you put in you.
no one can take away what you invest in yourself.

***

no one can take away what you invest in yourself.

how to invest in yourself. inventory your current intake. the music you listen to. the food you eat. the people you surround. the books you read. the work you do. the love you deserve. the hopes you have. then spend a good amount of time wondering where you see your life in a year from now. five years from now. ten years from now. twenty years from now. fifty years from now. a generation after you are gone from now. create a backwards plan to get there. go against the grain of what others tell you that you cannot do and do it. this doesn't just mean monetarily. it means spiritually. socially. emotionally. justicely. politically. religiously. nondenomenationally. agnostically. universally. lovingly. then do something. work towards that. and if the route changes adjust the plan or re-design the way the direction the reason the how as often as you would like to love.

a quick note on worry.

worry can sometimes grip you. consume and devour
every moment your mind takes a breath. calculating
what to say how to feel where to go what to do who to love.
it takes a toll. to the extent you undecide
decide undecide decide undecide decide undecide.
this is because you middle. you flow. you mediate.
wanting to ensure everyone is considered. everyone
is included. everyone is good. this is pure of you.
lover in you. giver in you. and know that it is okay.
and when you can try to worry less)not about being
you or being caring and kind(about your impact.
everything from you is the definition of love.

***

how can you discover what is already here. and how can you claim what is already theirs. that taking mentality has cursed and destroyed and ruined millions of lives. may the indigenous people specifically the tribes of bay miwok)chupcan, julpun, ompin, saclan, tatcan, and volvon(who communally owned the land in which i live on now in northern california be lifted. honored. remembered. compensated. on all days in all ways beyond land acknowledgments.

how to acknowledge indigenous peoples. change all the names all the streets all the neighborhoods all the mascots all the logos all the signs all the appropriations unless it is deemed okay and beneficial for them to remain granted by them and only them. research american indians and alaska natives. start there.

let your journey be yours.

people grow. and people stay the same.
it's not your responsibility to shame or
show off. let your journey be yours. let
their journey be theirs. concentrate on
your higher vibration and meet your
greatest self by recognizing that
you were once in the way
of what you didn't
know.

***

how to meet your greatest self. with patience. with ease. with homecoming and not why you took so long. with wide wonder of what it looked like seeing yourself do the things you did consciously and unconsciously to meet you where you are. with solidarity and appreciation for what it took you to take you to where you were meant to be when you get there. you'll know you got there when the stuff your old self used to trip over now feels mundane and doesn't trigger you.

longing for you.

and just like that. you are up again. out of a dark cloud. a place a feeling a reality that felt it would stay the same with no clearing in sight. but you)the way you do(stayed and did what was in your control. you stopped letting negativity passage its way through you. you changed what you let in. who you let in. how you let in. why you let in. and the clearing happened because you became clear. cleansed. rid yourself. focused on self. noticed who left and stayed gone and how much better you felt by not longing for their attention. you are the master of your growth and healing.

***

if you gotta force it then it wasn't meant to fit. but just because their ideal looks a certain way most often means that is outdated. but don't go where they don't appreciate you. they will just use you for their own needs then move to the next in thing. aware of that. beware of that.

how to not long for their attention. determine what excites you and not drains you. pour yourself something cold or warm and drink it or bathe in it. this cooling this warming is what you feel like to them. the coolness that refreshes. the hotness that soothes. focus in on that experience not because it is what they are missing but because sometimes you need to be reminded of what your attention fills like. what your love feels like. and know that what you bring is so important and valuable. you are important and valuable.

little big things.

that thing. that one small thing. the hello. the open
door. the hope you are well. the how's your heart.
the just in case i don't see you later. the picking
up a bouquet. the favorite artist came out with
a new banger music share. the thank you. the
i appreciate you. the thinking of you. makes
a difference. such a big difference. little
things. miniscule gestures. humanly
offerings. the missing links. you
do this. the meaningful stuff.
and it changes the course.
you change hearts.

***

you change hearts. and if that isn't magic.
i don't know what magic is.

pay it forward. you were given something. maybe not a lot in your eyes. but you were given something. rather than making it harder on someone else bring them ease. do the small things. doesn't have to be grand in size. the tiny things are what people remember. make them feel seen heard appreciated loved and you will have changed their life for good. for good. for. good.

how to be remembered for the little things. it's the detail of things that stand the test of time. the little things that signature you. mark you. favor you. in the grace of others. in the service of others. by seeing them without diminishing them. just always be kind.

new season fresh.

every day you outgrow something. some one. some
habit. some attachment. some pain. some crave. and
no longer want or need or care to have in your life
anymore. in your aura anymore. in your story any
more. but you feel obligated to hold onto and keep
and storage those belongings. those old connections.
those old memories. as obligation. as just in case.
as ties that are untied but boxed away to album and
look back one day. but you should know it is okay
)more than okay(to release. to unbind. to detach
from outgrown things that no longer serve you.
to wish well but go into your new season fresh.

***

you are allowed to do what is best for you. don't be held down by old things that no longer serve you support you love you grow you appreciate you.

what do you do when you outgrow clothes. some cut them to make them still fit. some put in the back of a closet. some give away for someone else to use and wear. those are phases of letting go. transitions can feel like treachery but sometimes you don't need to return to an old chapter when it's finished.

how to go into your new season fresh. practice gratitude in a way you may never have before. if you've done the three things you are grateful for each day ritual try bringing to mind one new person each rising and tell them one thing directly you are grateful for that they add to your life to your light to your space. fresh love acts new.

thoughts on showing up for your person.

if you really want to show up for your person.
ask them directly what they need and be that.
show that. try that. if it's outside your ability
see if there are other ways to provide support.
to present. to aware. to say. to do. to hold.
being there is about tending not dictating.
allowing not controlling. good hearts
listen and take what is heard and
turn messages into medicine.

***

good hearts listen and take what is heard
and turn messages into medicine.

learn to be there for someone how they need you to be there. showing up for someone doesn't mean bring them what you'd want to be given. ask how they prefer to be cared for. what it is they need. what would be helpful. if they say surprise me then surprise them. better to over check in and not to have checked in at all. your person needs you to know you will exceed their expectations because you care enough to not because it is the expectation.

how to ask someone what they need. listen. i know this keeps showing up. but listening is not something you just do. so much information buzzing around it can be hard to decipher and silence it especially while you're processing other stuff while listening to someone else talk. your mind is a powerful power. so another note on listening may look like this. grab hold to their last last word and don't let go. then say that word in a question to verify their need)s(.

all about trust.

when it doesn't feel right. trust that. trust you.
you might miss out on a short term feel good
but the long term feels better. when you rule
yourself and command greater treatment to
not fall not stray not revert not succumb to
previous patterns of putting people who
are poisonous to your very existence
back into your system back into
your galaxy then you persist.
you get better. you aren't
perfect but you deserve
flawless love.

***

day by day. day by day. could take a long while to get whatever and whoever out of your system and you may be hard on yourself for going back for falling back but get back and forgive yourself for being human. for give is the gap you need the brace you need the room you need to thrust you where you'll soon feel free. take your time but don't let anyone tell you you're foolish for bettering your life your world your galaxy. you are one choice away from the moment that will transform how you make the next decision and the next. practice the love you know you will grasp and keep your heart towards love. always towards love.

how to practice the love you know you will grasp. treat you best. not in comparison to others. but golden rule you too. provide the spread and the hole nine yards you would provide unto others and do it unto you. this sounds like you just heard something like this. you have. this reminder is just in case you skip straight to this page.

blossom into your next best version.

don't try. all. every. pour your you into love
into life into what you do. it is who you are.
half of you isn't the sum of you. the hum
of you is one thousand percent beautiful
but still not enough of you. many wait
to nitpick and look for faults in you.
cracks in you. flaws in you. to say
see you aren't all that. but you
are all that. your blemishes
are beauty marks. let them work
to undo you with gossip while you
blossom into your next best version.

* the lover in me honors the lover you in you.

***

next you talk about someone talk highly. talk goodly. talk of them of what you appreciate not the what they did to get under you skin unless under skin references the love you have for them. too much gossip not enough love. be the one that spreads love.

how to spread love. resist the urge to negative. to critique. to havoc. to get back. to one up. to ridicule. just positive. no not in the toxic positivity sense. life happens. it isn't always silver linings and rainbows. this is about preventing yourself from adding to the negativity there is already so much of. emit love by giving love. being love. it won't always come back to you the way you put it out love but you can't worry about that love. this love. your love. creates love. spaces love. endears love. manifests love. and it unlocks something in someone who catches on to your love to then pay it forward in their world love. if this is all you do then let spreading love be your main mantra. greet people in love by saying lovasté*.

four signs you are done done ready to move on.

you don't care anymore.
there is no room to grow.
priorities have shifted.
you aren't needed there.

change is hard. it takes work. it takes notice.
it takes time. it takes you. and you can't stay
in places and with people that stunt you.

so go. break. boundary. warn. address. stop.
figure out and feel it out. and if you are done
it is because you are ready for more love.

***

how to move on. use the law of two feet and literally go. walk away. use the law of four wheels and drive. far from that space. use the law of you and breathe in your dignity and stop making excuses for the situation for the person for the place to get better when it's been proven it won't it won't no matter no matter how much you try you change you adapt you accommodate you cut off your circulation for what would never do the same for you. trust that there is grand out there for you. better out there for you. homecoming out there for you. but you cannot one in one out. you must all in. all in. make all the plans you need. save all that you can save. take what you need and leave the rest with the rest. new flowers don't need to pick up old leaves. new flowers don't need to pick up old leaves. new flowers don't need to pick up old leaves. new flowers don't need to pick up old leaves. new flowers don't need to pick up old leaves. new flowers don't need to pick up old leaves. new flowers don't need to pick up old leaves. new flowers don't need to pick up old leaves. move on.

missing you means more than i love you.

i miss you already.
i miss you always.
i miss you now.
i miss you.

missing you means more than i love you.
missing you means more than i need you.
missing you means the connection we have
feels incomplete even if you are beside me.
missing you means come closer)closer
than close(and whole me. hold me.
in words. in acts. in love. in you.

***

the way you make someone feels matters. and the way you customize your love for each person is astonishing. how do you do it. how do you do that. ensuring every soul feels special. feels what they have been missing since always. don't tell me. don't tell me. show me. show me.

how to show love. not for show love. not for kudos love. not for did you see what i did for you love. you receptive to feedback love. you take a deep breath while they share with you how let down they feel when you did that thing love without tit-for-tatting back and forthing saying well-you-hurt-me-too thing you sometimes do love. that isn't love love. that is ego love. and we already noted about ego love. so just breathe love. show love. in the areas you tend to forget love. leave a message at the tone love even if they pick up the phone love. remind them why they chose you love. remind yourself why you love your love love. save this and come back later love.

to remind you when they forget.

you are beautiful. in the form of that sentence
you'd think no one would forget. that you would
hear the chamber of that statement everyday and
have it always hit your soul but it feels different
when those words are full. when sun shines at the
opening of you and clouds clear at the rounding
of are and the earth shakes)oh how the earth
shakes(at the source of beauty. when those words
land)really land(not as filler but as fact like seeing
love for the first time it carries you through.
but no matter you know you are brimming
with sunlight. everyone can't see magic.

***

you can't always wait to be seen. sometimes you have to go somewhere else to be appreciated. by then when they catch on you'll be long gone and they will wish they knew what they had from the very beginning.

how to remind you when they forget. know that everyone is human although you are more than human. know that there is nothing in you that needs modifying to keep someone who doesn't want to stay. know that being taken for granted means they know they have the world in you but are too immature to see the future in front of their eyes with you. know that beauty is a feeling that can't be replicated it is soul level that only those who speak the language can truly feel its aura its honor it's not on you to remind them when they forget. it's not on you to remind them they forget. it's not on you to remind them when they forget. if they forget they never truly knew.

ready. ready. ready.

if you keep waiting until you are ready
)when you think you are ready(it may
be too late. it will never be the right
time. the perfect time. sometimes
you just have to take a leap of
faith and courage and trust
that you will be okay.
that you will be
everything
you will
need.

***

when you don't have faith in you take a deep breath of you and dig into that part of you that you've been keeping on reserve. now is the time to use that courage. every time is your chance to believe in you more.

how to stay ready so you don't have to get ready. do what you are doing. at your best or near best or past your best. often. majority. as much as possible. what seems small is chance to prepare. chance to tinker. chance to prototype what you say you been wanting. each opportunity is a brick in your wall. each yes is the mortar. you stack your stack one at a time. all at once there is no foundation there is no discipline there is no foresight just huge appetite that will never be satisfied because you aren't doing it for any meaningful reason. so when the big break comes the big love comes the big wave hits you are prepared. you are collected. because you been there. you have been establishing. orienting. navigating. ready. ready. ready.

everything about you is a love hope.

acts of you. gifts of you. words of you.
touch of you. time of you. all of you.
the now of you should be proud of
you. should be wowed with you.
cuz i am. but my thoughts of
you keep circling on the
how you do what you do. how
the waters of you just flow like
you float. everything about you is
a love hope. everything. every
thing that touches you grows grows
grows the way of the lover. beautiful.

***

they can take what you do. the outside of it. copy it. copy you. but they can never take the soul of you. the heart of you. they may get far but they will not last. you are the secret they can not have.

how to know you are everything. just do. believe. trust. not to convince but to aware. to know is to attract. to know is to retain. to know is the embrace all that you are and you are everything and more. and more. and more. and more each time you know this knowing. know this knowing. know this inherently. not in boast but in self. assurance. self. admiration. self. content. self. amor. amor.

stay close to people that make you feel seen.

people who think of you.
people who reach for you.
people who fawn of you.
people who pray for you.
people who highly of you.
people who search for you.
people who madly of you.
people who wait for you.
people who dream of you.
people who best for you.
people who honor you
for you. deserve you.

***

stay close to people who make you feel seen. get further away from people who don't help you grow.

how to make people feel seen. say this. mean this. *i see you. i honor you. i acknowledge you.* not in a having power over talking under no this is a mirroring. an offering. a bowing. in reverance. in observance. to their person. their existence. their time. the times you felt witnessed reach back to that chapter to that memory to that filling. fill your person with that water. continuously. continually. ritually. carefully.

control doesn't look good on anyone.

control will block you. box you. stop you.
prevent you from receiving what has been
trying trying trying trying trying trying try
ing to get to you. so if you truly want what
is waiting for you. who is waiting for you.
let go. let go of rigid expectations to fit
molds not meant for you. let go of a love
not written for you. let go of changing
for someone who won't change for you.
unbind and undo what clings and clenches
you to turn you into someone who isn't you.
you are boundless. live outside the lines love.

***

let go of changing for someone who won't change for you. don't waste the energy. don't waste the love. don't waste the time. change is nothing when your heart is missing inside.

how to let go of control. trust. there goes that word again. let's break trust down. to trust means to submit to the will of what is not in your control. to surrender. to let go. to release control. so how do you let go. you trust. by accepting you did your part. that you did what you could. that you are willing to allow what will flow back in response if anything should come back. i hope something comes back. you deserve back. you deserve every bit of good. but whatever comes trust you can handle it. trust you can overcome it. trust you can embrace it. can't dictate the sun to come any closer or shine any brighter. but you can turn on your light and adjust your brilliance.

hope this one lands for you.

just because the wrong person got to you first
doesn't mean the right person has to make up
for their deficits. their shortcomings. their past.
but they can remind you of where you've been.
remind you what was worth climbing through
mud for. remind you why your smile smiles
so wide because they keep it for you in those
moments you lose track of it. and don't you
allow what didn't work cast a shadow on you.
you were always right. right right. beautifully
right. so that story in your head that says you
are broken is wrong. you are a gorgeous truth.

***

imagine how many smiles you are responsible for and multiply that by a million. you still wouldn't be close to the actual number of souls who are brighter because of you.

how to change the story in your head. recognize the story is there. whether it has been there for a day or a week or a month or a year or for some years this recognition isn't just about sensing its presence. this recognition is about sending its presence a notice. a changing of the guard. a telling that waves it away quicker than it arrived because it has out stayed and must be out by the end of this page so you can re-write your story your history your narrative you're not responsible for the deficits they had. you're not carrying their problems anymore as yours anymore. not any more. no more. remove the words the blame the deception they gave as your own and take hold of all the good all the positive all the compliments you once thought you didn't deserve. pin those to your heart.

let the past be past.

let the past be past and keep those not meant for you there. don't take that or them into your today and tomorrow anymore.

moving slow is still moving.

moving slow is still moving.

***

for when they tell you you're going slow. too slow. for when they tell you hurry up. for when they tell you pick up the pace. for when they rush you. this is what you know. this is what you tell them. tell them you can't rush through life. certainly can't rush anything about you.

but speed up freedom and equality. speed up the bonds of oppression that bond people that say heritage over hate. speed up the injustice system to see its darkness on marginalized people. rush to have better humans to make better decisions that have real life consequences.

how to speed up freedom and equality. you. get involved. you push and push and push and keep ensuring those that say they are leaders are leaders in that it helps those who have been diminished dismissed pushed out. ask open ended questions not because you already know the answers but because you don't have all the answers you are a mirror)a curious mirror(looking to see if they see what you see.

read this one slowly.

everyone gets in a funk. in a rut. in a daze that feels like it goes on for days. and yes you want to get out of it snap out of it to rejoin the feel good emotions rather than the not so good vibrations that have you off. have you out. have you on low. have you irritated at the world at the others at the one looking in the mirror. but it's ok. know that you are okay to be with what needs to be with. and that is all of you. you are all sides of a beautiful soul. the dark and the light. all of you is desirable.

***

when you accept all of you none of you bothers you. and nothing no one says has power to undermind underheart undersoul you. take you back. love you back.

how to love you back. you tell you. write here: how to love me back:

what did you come up with. were you honest. is it still blank. still looking for the how. a how. *love tip: do for yourself what others won't do or know how to do as good as you do. love you by taste not recipe.*

the deep breath you been waiting for.

don't sentence yourself to some one liner
someone posted and reposted and somehow
got to you compressed. smeared. pixelated.
words robbed of its soil. robbed of its maker.
robbed of its context. shortened to quickly
get into your system. then fade just as fast
as it came. because nothing about you is
instant. or abbreviated. or condensed. you
are the longest breath and the deepest verse
that never ends. your highlight reel has nothing
on your full clip. your fullness. you're absolutely
the most profound somebody to fully breathe in.

***

don't let anyone shorten you. silence you. abbreviate you. diminish you. just because someone did that to them doesn't mean they can do it to you.

how to know if you are being abbreviated. inventory your next 3-5 conversations. the amount doesn't matter just at least more than one. and just see how long it takes for the subject to turn from you to turn back to them. when the topic is on them let it be about them. be genuinely interested as you always are and do. then at your update at your news at your opening gauge their interest in you. do they ask follow up questions do they interrupt do they show support or excitement in the world of you. time it. in heartbeats or in clock. if they hit you with the that's cool and insert them you'll know. you already know. you are being abbreviated shortened cared less. bring it to their attention. see how they respond. do this for you. too. try this on to see if you make everything about you. too.

four do's they won't do for you.

do what they won't do. for you.
do what they deny you. for you.
do what they can't do. for you.
do what they want to. for you.

the space between waiting and now is you.
fill in the gap of you with you even when
you expect part of you to be embraced
by what and who that may never come.
this is so you are always complete without
relying on a rainbow with no gold. draw
from your own waters. quench your own thirst.

***

back when you want to. back when you come to. back when you feel to. in your absence it is the coldest winter coldest weather. but the heat of you lasts forever. your retreat is deserved and your arrival is a homecoming.

how to do for you. some people can be absolute in the way they live and love. some people make no allowance for gray area. but to know there is gray allows for more wondering and more compromise or at least more room to be messy instead of feeling the need to be right or on target or without blemish. doing for you can look like exploring the wilderness in you. understanding there is no end just more more. more of you. more territory to turn the light towards. realizing that the space between waiting and now is you. so decide where you want to go what you want to learn and go and learn and be the one you've been waiting for while whatever is for you makes its way to you.

the most beautiful where have you been
without saying where have you been.

finally. after all this time)time drags when you
aren't around(you are here. never lost. always
there. in the universe. in your own world doing
what you needed to. but seeing you hearing you
feeling you has been forever on my mind. where
has your heart taken you what has your soul seen
how are you holding the sky from falling because
your absence from mine causes gravity to leave
too. wherever you go love grows. wherever you
are i am. but this time stay longer. tell me
everything. tell me slowly. tell me
did you think of me as well.

***

where you have been has to be better. because of you.
the time of you. the space of you. the holding you
held didn't even want to be let go of because
it's you. the next where you attend will
be the next best tending that place
has ever experienced. and all
the beings present will
forever be better.

how to stay longer. turn off all the devices. no cameras. no phones. no notebook. no distractions. just be. dedicate yourself to that present. to that moment. to that once in a lifetime. you won't get that back. so get comfortable knowing the retell of that experience will be mixed with breath and sound and many hints of your sun.

ten treats to bring you joy.

treat yourself to outstanding love.
treat yourself to new experiences.
treat yourself to better relationships.
treat yourself to kinder environments.
treat yourself to overdue alone time.
treat yourself to what you crave.
treat yourself to learn more about you.
treat yourself to feel what you haven't felt.
treat yourself to more fun more happiness.
treat yourself to be who you want to be.

***

treat yourself better than anyone treats you.

treat yourself better. you are better when you choose yourself. to be yourself. to love yourself. to honor yourself. nothing selfish about self love.

how to treat yourself. without guilt or shame or apology.

they all hope it's you.

you have this graceful nature. a peaceful ocean
resides inside the swell of you. the coast of you
is soft breezes. gentle honey. the best kind of
sand and water. inland in you there is so much
freshness. green energy. strong roots. high sun
and deep treasure. islands like you are relics.
rare and beautiful. nothing in existence is like
you. you are the last autumn and the first spring.
not on a map or found easily you are off the
beaten path off the grid off the radar treading
surviving thriving wandering. they all hope it's
you that loves them back. if they ever find you.

***

how to be found without a map. accept that many will get lost looking for you. many are still lost. you can be in front of them in plain sight they can sense you are around but if they do not know what they are looking for and do not have the willingness to love you the way you need to be loved they will remain lost to you no matter how many signs how many passes how many reminders you flare they cannot see if they are too stubborn to know you can't be seen with eyes. to find you without a map there must be closing. there must be feeling. there must be critical looking inward. and there)there there there(you are. where you have always been.

the kind of unforgettable memory that lasts.

you will always be a necessary memory. one that beautifully haunts and taunts and takes over every nostalgic moment. every remember when. every wanting to go back to the first time that one time that right time that can we return and chill there how it used to be time. so when you get rocked and tell yourself that you are forgetten that you are not memorable. that you are nothing but a distant thought. stop. people can't go seconds without thinking of you. for you are unforgettable. a dream no one wants to wake from. you are the echo everyone hears and holds and holds and holds.

***

you are the repeated line. the dance break in every song. the hook that comes back comes back comes back. you are unforgettable. you are beautiful nostalgia.

how to last. choose you. search for inspiration in you. compass you. know the cardinal directions of you. declare what centers you. outward isn't bad but it is only bad if that is the only work you do. to last to sustain to longer takes commitment to self guide down the internal highway no matter the speed. slow. fast. bravely. timidly. innerly. that's time that pays dividends. that interests. that yields. the accumulation is the bounty that never decreases it just increases. always increases. as this is how monuments are built. how the pyramids forever.

an anti-hate statement.

whatever happens next week. next month. next four years. don't forget your humanity. your character. your love that love sends your way. we all have people we care about but no one life should suffer for careless lack of considering one another. you aren't lumped in a box. you can choose to be good and still disagree. but hate will never be welcome here. if you are on that side you will never be free. choose love. always choose love.

***

how to know you're on the side of good. the barometer)there are so many barometers(can be broken down to one consideration. who is at risk. under that risk assessment there is life. there is heart. the opposite of war is not anti-war or peace. the oppositive of war is care. is kind. is it too much to save lives instead of take lives from others that want to go home like you. it is said that the evil ones have a purpose have thoughts that what they are doing is in the name of good in the name of bettering in the name of humanity but no good can come from the extinction of someone because they are an iota different than you. the side of good must be measured differently.

look inward.

when you are lost. look inward.
when you need advice. look inward.
when you are down. look inward.
when you want love. look inward.
when you hurt deep. look inward.
when you overthink. look inward.
when you overfeel. look inward.
when you require more. look inward.
when you don't know. look inward.
when you are hopeless. look inward.
when you can't right now. look inward.
when you seek closure. look inward.

***

always look within. look inward. first. you'll find something. you'll find the someone you need. always. always. always.

how to inward. another way to look inward is to be hypersensitive to details. a redundant note but redundancy builds muscle memory like the way you can do what you can without having to consciously tell yourself to do certain things. perhaps your inward journey will be like those times you end up some place and wonder how you got there in the first place. this auto-pilot this automatic this practice can be uncomfortable at first especially for those used to running away instead of towards. but the goal isn't to get faster at something the goal is to be a bit more efficient in recognizing what you are meant to learn in that lesson at that moment in time. so one way to inward would be to embed one simple ask of yourself that may sound like this. what am i meant to learn or unlearn right now. and let that inquisition marinate and see what unfolds in the process.

love lessons.

forgive quicker. love longer. imagine more.
play intentionally. listen. express needs. ask
all the questions. hold hands. kiss for every
occasion. say thank you. appreciate family.
ask about friends. go outside. read books.
sleep in. enjoy moments. get what you
want. make bold choices. trust your
decisions. value closeness. you
embody life lessons. reheart
what it means to go with
love & love be enough
to be good and full.

***

you reheart what it means to go with love and love be enough to be good and full.

how to pinpoint a love lesson. you tell you. in the space below recall a memory a story a happening and pull out one of the insights.

even if it doesn't feel like love love has a message waiting for you.

twelve you should be's.

someone's first priority.
someone's first thought.
someone's first choice.
someone's first impression.
someone's first love.
someone's first everything.
someone's first crush.
someone's first song.
someone's first home.
someone's first forever.
someone's first smile.
someone's first wonder.

***

you should be because you are. every special thing. every little big thing. because you are more than deserving of the highest honor. the highest love. the highest appreciation. without lowering expectations.

how to never lower your expectations. choose you. rather than focusing on who doesn't like you focus on who deserves you. who loves you. who would root for you when you can't seem to root for you. keep the door open to see who dares step in. that doesn't mean give them everything it means give them a chance to come to their senses. you are someone's everything before and after they know it.

possible possibilities.

it's possible to let the small stuff go.
it's possible to have amicable disagreements.
it's possible to tune out unsupportive voices.
it's possible to love someone who doesn't love you.

it's not possible to live a better more meaningful life
without compromise. without understanding. without
care. from all sides. one-sided battles mean you are
the only one trying and that is unfair and intolerable.
some people just can't see beyond their own stuff.
their own interests. leave them be. take your love
elsewhere. just because it is possible doesn't always
mean you should keep wasting your precious energy.

***

you are the best possibility. the wildest reality. don't keep giving access to your well because the idea of them feels good. wait until they show you who they are before you give them every piece of you. keep you to you until they prove worthy.

and just because you would go above and beyond doesn't mean you should keep planting yourself in toxic soil. you know who to keep away from. you know who to give your love to.

how to love someone who doesn't love you. never again.

the five protections.

protect your peace. protect your heart.
protect your spirit. protect your being.
protect your love at all costs. because
whatever happens you must remember
that you have every right to engage or
disengage. surround or avoid. become
or break from. and if someone doesn't
understand or respect your boundaries
then it tells you your mental health is
not sacred to them)you are so sacred
beloved(you must protect your sacred
ness. you must protect your sacredness.

***

how to protect your sacredness. being up front some see it as brash. and it is. but not in the negative sense. in the important sense. to go in loosely as if inviting a joke of yourself doesn't give you the full freight of your seriousness. it is okay to be serious about your heart. if they cannot handle the frame of you how do you think they would treat the interior of you. so the next time be clear with who you are and what you are and what you are all about. no need to play small just to fit in anyone's back pocket.

you can't hear anyone that doesn't speak in love.

you can't hear anyone who doesn't speak in love.

for when you need this.

thinking of you. tonight. tomorrow. and all
the days before. and all the days that follow.
but especially now)right now(because i can
feel your body tighten feel your mind wander
feel your heart drop feel your hands tense.
what i want to do)what i always want to do(
is hold all of you. some of you. part of you.
whatever you need me to. to ease you. to
breathe for you. to water you. to remind you.
even if only a short while. the way you need.
you aren't alone even when you think you are.
i am there. with you. with you. i am with you.

***

you are thought of and dreamed of more than you know. even right now. even right now.

how to know you need this. on the heels of long endless stressful days that ache your bones and tense your shoulders and there is no patience left in you because the last mindful energy you could muster was to that last response you just gave a person you wish you could have really spoke your mind to but you had one last drop of grace and now and now and now there is some agitation some steam that needs blown off or else it tips to someone who doesn't deserve the tipping so instead this is the page you turn to block yourself from railroading someone who only wishes you well and wishes you love. this is to remind you that you need you to take ten minutes before entering a new space and prepare for transition. sit by yourself if you can and feel the tension leave you so you be gentle to those who deserve your petals and not your thorns.

another reminder to rest.

i feel the tension so give me yours.
not because you can't handle it but
because you deserve rest.

rest isn't too close to call. rest.
break isn't too close to call. break.
breath isn't too close to call. breathe.

it is normal to feel stressed.
it is normal to feel anxious.
it is normal to feel on edge.

so take what you need. be what you need.
do what you need. speak what you need.
you don't have to explain or defend.
it's okay if you're not okay.

you don't have to defend your rest or your break or your breath.
do what you need to do to be able to be okay. to be you. to be. you.

how to rest. II. when you have made the decision to walk away from something to reclaim center and get to air you haven't aired yet it might take a while to get your rest channel away from the busy occupied channel you just came from. either give yourself a permission slip that literally says you have permission to leave all that stuff where it is and when you get back all that stuff you left will be right where you left it. that could work. or set an alarm on your phone to go off the top of every or every other hour with a title that says yep it's okay if your mind just thought of that other channel now bring it back to the rest you were just resting. whatever works.

dear people who paused in june.

dear people who paused in june.
dear people who amplified in june.
dear people who listened in june.
dear people who muted in june.
dear people who unlearned in june.

what happened. where did you go. what did you forget. when you could not avoid you heard and couldn't believe and vowed to do your part to combat institutional racism and hatred and now the discomfort has gone away. this was the test. this isn't a once in a month thing. this is an everyday choice thing. what did you choose. you wanted to know what you could do how you could support how you could be better. the answer was crystal clear. temporary allyship isn't allyship.

how to stand in the fire and fight. black squares don't change lives. from the cries you heard from your fellow americans. from the bodies taken before your eyes. from the breath squeezed away on screen. from the rage and the sadness in the voices of your coworkers and students. did that feeling go away when it really mattered. did the care lose out to protecting a system steeped in white supremacist culture. not everything is perfect but you can't stand by hate and none of it not get on you. you still have work to do but when folks tell you they are tired of waiting this is why. may you never ever ever ever ever have to daily experience a system against you. other humans against you. other laws against you. and for you to have to defend yourself and fight for yourself and do all the things to try and live. imagine the privilege it is to not have a worry about experiencing trauma but only having someone just tell you about theirs. imagine.

two types of trying to be done trying.

be done trying to convince people. be done trying to make them see. make them hear. make them feel. some are too far gone. don't lose yourself trying to get anyone unwilling to see the beautiful humanity in you.

***

how to be done trying to convince people. value your energy at its highest rate. beyond the market rate. name your own price skyrocket it high enough that you are in a galaxy of your own. this way no one can compare you)they can't compare you anyway(to any other. and then triple it. infinity it. that is how valuable you are. and people who you have to convince otherwise aren't allowed near your energy if they ask you who you think you are.

how to be done trying to make them see. keep your light on. never turn your light off. no need to block them or restrict them or change how you move because they are somewhere near your lane with mutual friends and groups and networks. no need to go elsewhere in order for them to then realize what their eyes couldn't appreciate. keep doing what you are doing. be done adjusting your brilliance and remain as brilliant if not more)there is no limit to your brilliance(. when you stop trying they may then do the trying the poking the initiating the missing the checking the stuff you been trying to get them to do for so long. but your stopping your being done wasn't and isn't to get them to suddenly bring you to awareness. your stopping and being done is for you to prepare for what is to come. and what is coming is far greater far better far more interested than the circumstance that can't even see you as you are. what can see you is craving you to close that unseeing door.

the worst kind of person.

the worst kind of person tells you they love you
in front of your face but behind your back does
everything possible to slander you. block you.
hide you. poison you. and when you come to
them. sharing your sorrows your successes
your experiences they use you against
you but you lift them you benefit them you
celebrate them. no matter what hardships hit
you hardest. you put you aside. but some
)the ones you think you know best(can't
do the same. some friends aren't your friends.
take inventory. you have every right
to clean out your closet.

***

how to clean out your closet. scan all your inventory. all your inventory. what is old that you say you are holding on to just in case you need it for that thing that occasion that may never come. unbox all the drawers and dressers and lay everything in front of you and scan further. probe deeper. consider your emotional ties your soul ties your reasons why you have what you have and if it is necessary to keep or disregard. is it the memory or the physical thing. the toxic thing or the healthy thing. the wanted thing or the needed thing. if it adds to your life keep it in your life if it detracts from your life remove it from your life. the quantity of a thing isn't important as the quality of the thing. the richness of the thing. the hope of the thing. the healing of the thing. thank whatever you are cleansing and ridding. thank whatever you are remaining and staying. soon more will come. soon more will need to be scanned.

a checklist. a heartlist.
to see how you are doing.
to see how we are doing.

do i honor you enough.
do i water you enough.
do i see you enough.
do i touch you enough.
do i hear you enough.
do i ask you enough.
do i lift you enough.
do i help you enough.
do i affirm you enough.
do i know you enough.
do i fill you enough.
do i love you enough.

your heart is more beautiful than you think it is. bigger than you say it is. needed more than you think it is.

***

how are you doing. how are we doing. not a quick good and go. but a slow how and how. to loop back and follow through. fill in. take out. dig in dig in. to care to check in. to think about more than once in awhile. but now. and now. but now. and now. and again. and again. and again. tell me. tell you. tell us. to not just be good. but to be fulfilled. and to know deep deep love.

how to meaningfully check-in. ask if they have time. not about studies or work or the shallow. but to dive together about the deep. about the condition of your together. then ask these. then ask these.

if they want easy that isn't you.

love is difficult. but when you have someone
willing to get in the trenches with you for you
while you figure your stuff out love becomes
a journey. but when anyone tells you that you
are too difficult. that you are too demanding.
that you are too much this tells you they are
on their way away from you. perhaps not
ready for the complexity of you. the roots
of you. you are not a fairy tale love. if they
want easy that isn't you. you are real and real
love comes with roll up your sleeves sit down
dig deep stand in the fire to stay in love. love.

***

your love isn't difficult it is deep. if they knew you they'd know the quickest way to your heart is to learn to dig for your beautiful roots.

how to get in the trenches. with conviction and determination knowing that you are all-in. and all-in carries only one condition. and that is to be all-in. together-in. completely in. all hearts in. for this to work through thick and thin in. trench in. stay in. when it gets hot in. the only running away is running towards in. carry your reservations and lets have a discussion. lean in. can't turn back now ride this until the wheels fall off in. all four seasons. if you can't be in be honest with your person before you lead them on in.

nine types of love you deserve.

merciful love. kind and compassionate.
unconditional love. without limits and restraint.
hopeful love. inspiring and optimistic.
curious love. full of wonder and adventure.
faithful love. loyal and true.
lasting love. always and enduring.
beautiful love. enhancing and memorable.
courageous love. brave and unwavering.
patient love. calm and understanding.

real love isn't shallow or convenient. it takes time to nurture. you can't rush intimate relationships.

***

you don't need to be reminded of how beautiful you are but even mirrors sometimes need someone to hold them up to the light.

love takes work. but if you aren't willing to re-evaluate and adjust and grow you should know why things don't eventually go as you hope. gotta be around for the valleys and not just the peaks. both remind you why you picked them. why they chose you. who you are and who you can be. you just have to practice love. you just have to practice.

how to practice love. with sincere willingness to lose your breath. lose all sense to make room for possibilities beyond your current imagination. this kind of expansion allows love to discover new love. new language. new hopes. new ways you never knew before.

seven ways to eliminate self-doubt.

stop seeking outside approval.
pinpoint how you are feeling.
start trusting your decisions.
pinpoint the source.
look for recurring patterns.
be compassionate with yourself.
doubt your doubts.

doubts are fears that feel real because
you experience them. they can keep you.
they are triggers that give you information.
train yourself to notice them and persevere.

***

doubt is that slow creeper. that inner critic telling you nah. stop. don't go any further. you shouldn't do that. can't do that. but you have to change the narrative. get rid of that tape that story that old recording and speak through whatever tries to trap you. wherever you want to go you can get there. just believe in yourself. believe despite what you may have been tricked to never think could be possible.

how to do any of the seven ways to eliminate self-doubt. in no particular order. choose one that presents as something you feel pulled to do interested in doing compelled to spend time stepping into that action that opportunity for as long as you are interested. if you are used to stopping when things get hard then don't allow yourself to stop on that action. stay there in that action a bit longer before moving into another way to eliminate.

the greatest imprint.

the greatest imprint is the one you leave. the one
that feels the same as if it just happened yesterday.
you are every today. every gentle memory lodged in
heartbeats. the one reason one rises up early
just to see you come up. to be covered in your
loving energy. in your light. the being you are
the beam you are the beauty you are is what will
always be remembered. for you are the greatest
feeling. for you are the greatest imprint. always
keep choosing you. for you are the reminder
everyone needs. for you are the sweetest breath.
the day only begins when you emerge.

***

how to leave an imprint. who are you now and who do you want to be. how do you make people feel now. how do you want to make people feel always. within your answers work backwards and select behaviors and phrases and ventures that align with that. to leave anything you would want to leave it better than you found it. so whatever you leave behind when you are no longer around is fond is fair is remarked what good you gifted what good you believed in what good you created. and if what you are doing now)i am sure it is solid and beautiful(but it can be turned up a bit. so give a bit more effort a bit more heart a bit more you and the intention will spill over. what is the one thing you want to be known for. journal that. sticky note that. breathe that. and then do that. completely. humbly. gently. and continually weigh it against your values re-visit your values what are your values as they will become the words the traces of you. you are a working document. peace be your journey.

you are loved.

you are loved despite the mistakes you make.
you are loved for that heart in your chest.
you are loved because you deserve to be loved.
you are loved regardless of being hard to reach.
you are loved even if you think you are not.

you are loved.
you are loved.
you are loved.
you are loved.
you are loved.
you are loved.
you are loved.
you are loved.
you are loved.
you are loved.
you are loved.
you are loved.
you are loved.
you are loved.
you are loved.
you are loved.
you are loved.
you are loved.
you are loved.
you are loved.
you are loved.
you are loved.
you are loved.
you are loved.

twelve ways to push yourself through hard times.

push yourself to take deep deep breaths.
push yourself to schedule time to rest.
push yourself to surround yourself with love.
push yourself to be overly kind with yourself.
push yourself to acknowledge all your emotions.
push yourself to cry instead of holding back.
push yourself to speak your heart language.
push yourself to share that you're struggling.
push yourself to focus on what is in your control.
push yourself to prioritize healthy relationships.
push yourself to practice daily gratitude.
push yourself to not push yourself and just be.

***

you are what you need. sometimes you just have to push yourself to remember what it is like to be beautifully human. even when you are down just know it is normal to have to rejuvenate. to soon be up again. if you aren't okay that's okay. the goal of life isn't to always be happy. the goal of life is to learn how to be you and help others learn themselves.

how to be okay with not being okay. life isn't perfect they say. and life has its battles they say. but no one prepares you for the down times just that you'll recover and be back up times they focus more on the getting back to and less on the processing where you are if you're not okay times. so when you are low or nothing is going your way or you are feeling sad and down and down and down don't think anything is wrong with you. it is your soul telling you you need some time with you. stay with you as long as you need.

where you'll find love.

when you discover your light
it will be where it has always been
inside you where most people look last.
that is where you'll find love.
that is where you'll find depth.
that is where you'll find meaning.
that is where you'll find courage.
that is where you'll find possibility.
that is where you'll find treasure.
go there. stay there for as long as
you need. find yourself more often.

how to find love. you stop looking for it.

how to find depth. you keep being curious.

how to find meaning. you always wonder why.

how to find courage. you take fear with you.

how to find possibility. you don't settle.

how to find treasure. you close your eyes.

how to discover your light. you talk to your shadows and your blindspots and your vulnerabilities and turn what you were told were thorns into buoys into light houses into wind so that you sail onward instead of anchored. you notice that all you do all you surround all you water grows. because of your light. because of your light. your light is just you choosing to stay afloat even in the dark.

you are a beautiful love.

you are beautiful love
because you are you love.
a dreamer. a peacemaker.
a healer. a whole heart language
harmonizing with the universe.

let go of souls who just don't care.

not saying you should give up. but doing the work
for two leaves you burnt out on a lost cause. and
sometimes you need to let go of souls who just
don't care. it's okay to let them go. keep yourself.
it's okay to choose a difficult path when it is easier
to stay in their pain. in their patrol. in their problem.
to wait for them to change but by the time they get
it together)if they ever get it together(you will have
been who you have always been. a giver.
a benefactor of grace. a lover who tried to save
something unsaveable. that's you. a fighter. but
you deserve someone who will fight for you, too.

***

you are a lot of things to a lot of people. the heartthrob and the mindthrob. you are the best kind of person to always think of.

move on from those that give you half love. move on from those people. move on from those places. move on from those practices. move into what you said you would always do. into what is no longer tolerable. anything under your expectations or against your boundaries are no longer welcome. doing that is beautiful selfishness. it makes you better. it fills you better. you deserve better.

how to let them go and keep yourself. practice beautiful selfishness. it looks like knowing it is hard to step away from someone but deciding to step towards you is more important no matter how much it hurts. can't make anyone do anything but you can make you be the one who saves you from more uneven heartache. tell yourself this is difficult but has to happen for your own heart health.

only full love for you love.

you are that long-term love. that forever always
infinity kind of love. that keep you up wondering
if you're still up kind of love. that where have you
been i've been searching what feels like a lifetime
kind of love. that right time kind of love. that look
yourself pinch yourself it may never happen again
kind of love. and just like anyone you sometimes
do the human thing and compare yourself to others
or wish you had something more about you that
would set you apart making the choice to choose
you easier. have you looked at you. have you felt you.
have you studied the history of you the stars
of you the magic of you. move on from those
who give you half love. who make you feel less.
only full love for you love.
only full love for you love.

how to reject half-love.

just like that.

thank you for getting you to you.

thank you. thank you for getting you to you.
thank you for holding onto you a little bit longer.
thank you for betting on yourself for telling yourself
you would make it because you had no other choice.
thank you for trusting you even though you may not
have always trusted you. look how far you've come.

***

how to trust yourself. the word trust is in this volume countlessly. as it is fundamental. as it is a skill and as in any skill it can be learned can be taught can be practiced)needs to be learned taught and practiced(as it is too often being unlearned unconsciously which counteracts its strength its importance its levity and necessity for anything any relationship any encounter trust is bedrock. i said it but i will say it again that trust must be earned but you shouldn't be going back and forth with trusting you. it will happen. the wavering. the teetering. the tottering. as you master new heights but your main flex should be mantra in the trust you have in yourself to see something through. to see you through. all the people can trust you but if you don't trust you you'll forever keep yourself in a limbo in a fugue state not really knowing who you are as you constantly call yourself into question. trust yourself by having a reason. having reasons. having resolve. the questions from others about your why may push you to defend what you are doing but if you know your why then let the questions come. even if your why is shaky you can establish that right now you're still figuring it out figuring you out but that your belief in your process in your developing is the route is the reason is the resolve to tighten the bond you have with you. again it's not about being right or perfect it's about having the capacity and courage to try and face what needs to be faced.

you're one of a kind. II

sometimes they will look for you in others
 and they won't find you. you're one of a kind.
sometimes they will stumble over their words
 trying to approach you. you're one of a kind.
sometimes they will forget what they have
 that's their biggest loss. you're one of a kind.
sometimes they will hold you from yourself
 go your separate ways. you're one of a kind.
sometimes they will make you think you're the
 problem but you're not. you're one of a kind.
sometimes they will underestimate how deep
 and how loving you are. you're one a kind.

***

don't forget. you're one of a kind.
one of a heart. one of a soul.
one of a beauty no one should
ever let go.

how to remember you're one of a kind. not in boast not in brag not in comparison to any other not in material not in monetary not in anything but radiating love being love showing love daring love sharing love spilling love loving love embracing love making love trusting love giving love growing love healing love kinding love kindling love being love be love. just be love.

the seven detachments.

detach yourself from people unworthy of you.
detach yourself from places unworthy of you.
detach yourself from thoughts unworthy of you.
detach yourself from worries unworthy of you.
detach yourself from energies unworthy of you.
detach yourself from distractions unworthy of you.
detach yourself from paths unworthy of you.

you always have the power
to detach yourself from
what no longer
serves you.

***

because you are you everything will be as it should. just remove what no longer serves you and you'll fly even higher.

how to detach yourself from what no longer serves you. honor that season the seasons this season that claimed your heart your energy your time your blessing and dig a ritual hole or a real hole and place something into it. you decide what the something is. set a time and set a timer to peace it and peace it then go in peace from it. go on to the next season knowing you gotta do what you gotta do to get you where you deserve to be. that you respectfully no matterly held on for as long as you had to as long as you could and now the new life new love new bloom is about to boost you where what shackled you couldn't jet you to. take no animosity with you for if you do it is still with you. can't go on fully until you're at peace. peace takes time so the willingness to piece it from you is a start.

six beautiful reminders for reminders.

loving things flow in your direction.
stand in your own wind you will not fall.
being strong is the softest thing you'll do.
slow of you is deep of you let them wait.
change can't always be seen but it is felt.
your love is contagious a beautiful home.

you are the reminder. the cue. the turn to.
the best kind of warning that shouldn't ever
have to question your holy. even storms have
to storm just to feel its rain. to feel its power.
to feel its motion. you)wild storm(are the
perfect weather.

***

even storms have to storm just to feel its rain. to feel its power. to feel its motion. you)wild storm(are the perfect weather.

how to storm. stormingly. youly. only you know how to. how to gather how to flow how to fly how to fall how to thunder how to pour how to wind how to sun and do it all again. your nature is yours. no one can tell water how to water. so be all the forms of water that you are as perfect as you are and grow yourself into as many oceans as many moons as many skies you want to.

you at half is still full.

you beloved soul are attractive. in ways this
language can't harness. so stay you. your heart
is a necessary remedy for souls in healing. for
souls in longing. for souls without you feel
unwhole unwell unappreciated unloved.
it's like you fill others without knowing how.
without needing to know how. it's just you.
and you should give that same unknowing
energy to you. don't feel obligated to always
make yourself available while in rest. it's okay
to need to to want to to have to well yourself. you
at half is still full. but you at full are remarkable.

***

how to remain full. by filling others. by fueling others. in ways you already do. by seeing them. by hearing them. by loving them. in doing so you get replenished. as if loving one is like loving a million souls. so just one. just one beloved. and you will have saved an entire generation of broken of wanted of forgotten of unloved of deserving)all deserve your kind of love(and love conspires back to you. repays you. refills you.

you are more.

you are not your past. you are more.
you are not your wounds. you are more.
you are not your mistakes. you are more.
you are not your insecurities. you are more.

you are all the things you need. and more.
you are all the things you hope. and more.
you are all the things you want. and more.
you are all the things you love. and more.

may you always breathe deeper and bolder.
you are beyond what anyone has ever told you.

***

you are more. you are always more.

how to accept that you are more. tear this page out or copy down all the words or one of the phrases and carry it with you. on you. tattoo them. absorb them. pocket them. clench them. breathe them. be them. memorize them. memorize you. and if ever your past your wounds your mistakes your insecurities bubble up speak these words back to them. you are not your past. you are more. you are not your wounds. you are more. you are not your mistakes. you are more. you are not your insecurities. you are more. you are all the things you need. and more. you are all the things you hope. and more. you are all the things you want. and more. you are all the things you love. and more. you are beyond what anyone has ever told you. you are more. you are always more.

this part is meant to turn you into gold.

this part is meant to turn you into gold.
don't ignore the lesson. don't reject your
blessing. if you forget)don't forget(you
are being stretched and sharpened and
yes you can be emotional. yes you can
feel resentful. yes you can be confused.
yes you don't have to have all the answers.
yes you are permitted to complain and yes
you will still become what you put your
heart and mind and effort to. so collapse
when you must collapse. embrace the journey.
you will rise because you are made of fire.

***

how to stand in the fire. don't go back to normal. that normal was a mirage. a facade. a trap. a guise. a front. a mask. a mask. a mask. don't put it back on. center what you centered then. work on what you were working on. and face the person you've been needing to see. the now can be challenging as you feel the pressure you feel the heat but you are heat too you are pressure too so heat back and pressure back and do not buckle if you don't want to buckle. if the stay is worth the result you are hoping for then stay and go on all cylinders but if it truly isn't what you want then reserve your fierce for another day another worth fiercing for. fire isn't meant to burn you fire is meant to golden you golden you golden you not exhaust you. not dismantle you. not frighten you. not contain you. stand in your fire in moments you don't think you have fire or are fire) you are fire(and raise your temperature rise your temperature rise dear fire.

six pillow talk questions.

what piece of you is hurting.
what past of you is denying you.
what peace of you is balancing you.
what passion of you is filling you.
what purpose of you is waking you.
what prayer of you is helping you.

***

when you heal others heal. a healing you is an inspiring you. don't underestimate the essence of you. the everything of you. the magic of you.

you are the silent prayer people speak to their pillows out their windows up to the stars with open hearts. your name sits on the lips of so many because you represent love. because you are love. because you are loved.

how to stop underestimating you. refer to page 84. and then begin to overestimate you. overtrust you. not in the sense of overinflating but in the boosting. in the super elevation to hype you. pride you. concentrate on exaggerating your essence so it lingers like a trail to find yourself again. to remind yourself that underestimating you is the worst thing you can do because it tells you that you don't believe you don't think you don't allow yourself a chance except for when you know you can set the standard become the standard be damned to be told you can't do something especially from yourself that cannot happen unless you've prepared to make the attempt and it isn't feasible. take responsibility for what you tell yourself love.

happiness is homemade.

happiness is homemade. and happiness is also a pursuit. a getting to. a process that isn't idle. and there will be times you will hear others tell you to be happy. as if it means to simply place a smile on your face or get that money or get that person or get that success and that will be all that you need. but what happens when you reach those things and still feel emptiness. still feel void. still feel incomplete and isolated. it means those things weren't enough and you were chasing values that didn't belong to you. it means evaluate what is important to you and what it is that you need to be fulfilled. then be that. do that. seek that. embody that. practice that. your happiness is an internal dialogue. it asks: *what am i grateful for? what am i grateful for?* for gratitude is the key in your homemade recipe.

outlets that once brought you joy or brought you peace can be hard to come by right now. you can want more or be bored of the same practices or truly miss that chemistry in person that connection that human contact to help you feel like you. to bring you back to center. but you are human and when humans feel confined and locked in they feel a loss of control. you know this. but this is about letting go of what you can't control and reminding you to think of the little things that holds your smile. that blushes your skin. that soothes your wonderful being. so to you beloved just remember. remember to tell someone how you feel about them. that will make your day by reminding them of them. remember to give because givers are filled by giving. remember to love because you are loving by nature. that is your path to happiness. that is your path to you.

how to pursue happiness. place your hand on your heart and vow to do what makes you happy and become the happiness you find.

selfish of you.

it is selfish of you not to set boundaries. it is selfish of you not putting you first. it is selfish of you not acknowledging what you won't put up with anymore. for so long they had their way and you kept quiet kept accepting kept coming back. be selfish in how you take back your self love.

***

it's okay to be selfish in how you take back your self love.

how to set boundaries. put you first.

how to put you first. set boundaries.

you shouldn't have to

lose sleep over people not losing sleep over you.
try so hard to get someone's unloving attention.
remind anyone that you deserve to be a priority.
explain or defend your right to be as you are.

you should

show up for you in your grand. in your truth.
and if anyone tries to diminish you gaslight you
lower you they can't. they can't. for love is what
rules you. guides you. grounds you. if they aren't
dripping in love they don't need to be around you.

***

love is what rules you. guides you. grounds you. if they
aren't dripping in love they don't need to be around you.

how to gaslight someone back. you don't. you're better than that. you know what it is like for someone to make it sound like what you are doing or feeling is invalid is your fault isn't real so why would you pass that ridicule on to someone else)you won't you don't(so when it is your chance to respond)if you have the energy(apologize for the person that hurt them. tell them you don't know what happened in your past that made them so harsh so rigid so robotic so head in the sand but you wish them love that they never experienced and hope they find a heart that hearts them back but will not stand for the hate the anger the sadness the demeanor they are demeaning towards you as you know it isn't about you. can't let them force you to gaslight someback. break that cycle with love.

where to go.

go where your fullness is celebrated.
go where your heart feels at home.
go where your everything is validated.
go where your sorrows are held.
go where your body is respected.
go where your giving is sacred.
go where your days are listened to.
go where your quiet isn't judged.
go where your inner peace is considered.
go where your heart language is understood.
go where your person is applauding you.
go where your spirit rises and rises and rises.

***

home feels like you. is you. and no matter how far)no matter how far(knowing you is knowing home away from home.

how to go where you're appreciated. with pleasure. with joy beaming from your chest you're not obligated to stay around toxic fumes. you're obligated to protect yourself from toxic fumes.

your vulnerability makes you beautiful.

your vulnerability makes you beautiful.
it is your openness and your courage to
face the hardest hills and the steepest
valleys not knowing the outcome.
but knowing whatever happens
you didn't compromise you.
you didn't sabatoge you.
you didn't go against
who you are. for
being you and
loving you
is brave.

***

for being you and loving you is brave. it is why so many)so so many(run to you. magnet to you. confide in you. trust in you. because you are the love marker. the greatest of all time. the horizon's horizon. the ocean's ocean. the stars star. keep lighting up the world. keep lighting up the world.

how to be vulnerable. locate the walls you have built. measure the length and the width and the height. see if you are able to timeline when each brick or stone or mountain or crag or slab was laid separately or all at once just so you can determine different points the wall was walled. decide which piece you're willing and able and interest to discuss with yourself or someone else. you can be detailed or broad. if it is hard to talk about say it is hard to talk about. name a feeling. describe the wall or part of the wall or none of the wall. do this little by little. wall by wall. share some of you.

now is the time.

now is the time to put you first.
now is the time to love you first.
now is the time to trust you first.
now is the time to follow you first.
now is the time to bet on you first.

and when you hesitate)the way you tend to do(
remember that givers always give and give and
often feel the weight of being there for everyone
even for people who don't deserve it. they don't
deserve you more than you deserve you. so give
you to you. firstly. humbly. lovingly. promptly.

how to know that now is the time. it is already overdue. can never be overdone when the first is rarely you. you know the time is now just by the energy around you that is left for you isn't enough to breathe in to feel rested for the next day that is bound to deplete you. when you're tired of making excuses for when you'll do something for you. in your hour of you has been taken over one too many times and haven't had your hour for you. that is when. that is now.

four realizations.

realize how necessary you have always been.
realize how much people light up around you.
realize how safe you make others feel.
realize how special your love really is.

and by realizing your worth your value your you
the nonsense falls away. the desire to entertain
unhealthy energies falls away. the need to please
those who don't spend seconds thinking of you
falls away. the focus on what is important goes
way up way up way up way up. higher. higher.
the season of you is about reclaiming all of you.

***

you at the center doesn't mean you don't care about others. you at the center means you're no longer keeping yourself on the margins.

how to bring yourself to center. repeat the four realizations until they actually become realized. then as you feel yourself drifting or being pushed from center back to margin you reclaim this. you reclaim you. you won't let it happen like they want it to happen so what has to happen is you stop apologizing for thinking you are taking up space and declare belonging in every space you occupy.

they can't tell your story.

they can say whatever they want about you. they can feel whatever they want about you. but they can't tell your story.

what you are

a giver. selfless. available. attentive.
a lover. thoughtful. compassionate. deep.
a warrior. loyal. trustworthy. committed.
a healer. present. kind. aware.

what you are not

someone's second choice. someone's last resort.
someone's convenience store. someone's rebound.
someone's one-sided benefit. someone's secret.
if at one glance they can't see your legendaryness.
your rawness. your fullness. they can't have you.

***

if at one glance they can't see your legendaryness. your rawness. your fullness. they can't have you. *highlight that. underline that. seriously. you can't move on until you mark those words somehow.*

how to highlight you. if you were too stubborn)it's okay to be stubborn(and didn't star or bold or circle or underline this is me doing it for you. repeating this for you. because you are legendary. you are legend. the legend. the map that contains the world and all of its stars and the stars yet to be starred. the giver the lover the warrior the healer in you is once in a lifetime so it is obligatory to call you out to you. directly. one more third to go in this book and there is still so much to share about you to reflect about you to tell about you and the surface still hasn't been scratched. so before you go on flip back and see what words you elevated what themes you uncovered what questions you have what tools have been helpful. what tools do you still need. and prepare yourself for more of you.

dodging heartache.

not everyone is for you but they will regret underhearting you. disregarding you. it's not their fault. you dodged their heartache.

the kind of people to fall in love with. II

fall in love with the kind of people who
call just because you are their because.
who don't make you lose who you
are but help find more of you. who
hype you for your small wins and
support you through hard moments.
who remind you of your magic when
your light starts to flicker. who show
you a love you don't have to ask for.

***

you are the best kind of because. and all the reasons why. the love that fills. the light that feels. the most beautiful heart there is.

how to fall in love with a person like you. deeply. intentionally. and if you share this book with a person you want to be your person bookmark this page for this to be the first to begin with. for to love someone like you there must be preparation. preparation for the unexpected. preparation for love and blessing. preparation for a love that stays and deeps and heals and alls.

the kind of person you already are.

be that person you can be proud of. that person you can say wasn't making life hard for others but was paving a path for future generations. that person that grace finds easily. that person that people can breathe more beautifully and deeply and genuinely because you inspire them to. that person who doesn't project onto others but notices there is still stuff to examine. that person who encourages vulnerability by being vulnerable. you are already this person. this was just to remind you.

***

your story is the best story. a triumph story. a deep story. a love story. a tale about a soul who always knew where they were going because they believed in each step they took. a tale about a lover with so much courage in the midst of those who would try to strip it from them. they are still trying. they still aren't stopping you.

how to tell your story. how you want to. as much as you want to. to who you want to. just because someone shows interest doesn't mean they get the full you. you can drip you. slow you. some you. or all you. up to you. open book. closed book. cracked book. secret book. your story is yours. tell it how you feel it. with details or vagueness. but never downplay. never under it where you make you think you aren't worthy of telling you. you are no one to compare to. so perhaps start with the story of your name and if you don't want to or don't know it you can create the story that feels right to you.

get away from unaccountable people.

if you can hold yourself accountable
own up to your part take responsibility
without re-directing it towards others
it is clear you are mature. clear you
aren't above error. clear you can
admit what went wrong and
plan to make it better.

it takes a special nature a special person a
special humility to stand in blame stand in heat
stand in judgment and stay. to hear. to humble.
to heart. and strive to love that much harder.

***

accountability looks good on you.

how to be accountable. rather than get defensive get open. breathe through what you didn't do. own up to your role. and no matter if you don't agree with their response you can control your response. with humility and heart.

if they leave while you change. II

if they leave while you change
they will have missed out
on knowing your better version.

if they leave while you change
don't hold grudges in your heart
there is so much life waiting
for you to go on go on grow on.

***

how to grow on if they leave while you change. remember. not everyone can go with you or will want to go with you. your daring your light your love is never before seen. and what people don't know they step away from. you're not for everyone. you're not for everyone. whatever they taught you you take with you. to lesson to lessen to less in when you would normally give in because not all compromise is fair. everyone won't last. but you will. but you will. and you grow on by finding the balance you once had before them or hand while with them and lodge within you to crutch you so you don't need to reach for a half or a part of anyone else to be complete. it is a special filling when another adds to us but you should overflow yourself and refill yourself. they can be icing but you gotta be the cake. the ingredients. the foundation. this doesn't mean you don't need anyone else. this doesn't mean you don't need anyone else. it means you need you. it means you complete you. it means you have to know the parts of you. the great of you. the why of you. the pull of you. you are the lock and the key.

once in a lifetime love.

you are the kind of soul
someone is striving for.
building for. wishing for.
hoping for. breathing for.
bettering for. digging for.
being for. whying for.
living for. loving for.
waiting for. smiling for.
crushing for. blushing for.
praying for. fighting for.
staying for. elevating for.

***

you are the kind of soul someone is looking for. waiting for. being for. when you find a once in a lifetime love like you that is the price. that is the duty. that is the reason. you're worth all the forring. worth all the forring.

you are the first they want to see. they don't say it now but they feel it now. they hold it now. in their nights. in their days. the love you're about to step into is coming. is there. has arrived. arriving.

how to treat a once in a lifetime love. spiritually. with gratitude and knowledge that you are living history as history is being written as records are being broken as muses muse. if you do that)if you tend to the roses the bougainvilleas the sunflowers as light reflecting light in there here and now instead of after or when it is too late then you won't miss wonder in action won't miss once in a lifetime love. because you will be able to count all the ways you love them instead of being distracted. pay attention. tend to your rare garden.

twelve reasons.

be the reason you look to.
be the reason you were made for.
be the reason you show up for.
be the reason you need to carry on.
be the reason you slow slow down.
be the reason you don't give up.
be the reason you quit bad habits.
be the reason you put up boundaries.
be the reason you heal old wounds.
be the reason you follow your heart.
be the reason you are whole.
be the reason you know love.

you are all the reasons that enrich life. you care. deeply. you kind. sincerely. you love. unbelievably. stay like this. stay like you.

***

and just when they think they've got you figured out you show another side of you that rattles them. when they figure out you're not to be figured out then they might have a fighting chance to get near your beautiful heart.

how to get near your beautiful heart. without rushing. with no rush. in the age of instant gratitification everyone wants things now seconds before now. but the ones willing to peace and wait and peace and wait and piece and weight little by little as the unfolding of you and them then getting to your center becomes and was the initial intent. not to pillage or break or leave but to breathe in breathe in breathe in breathe in and be a witness to all the magic beautiful hearts are made of.

thirteen things to always remember.

everyone won't see what you see.
impact matters more than intent.
you can disagree and still get along.
asking for help makes you stronger.
we're all healing from something.
you won't always get it right.
if you listen you unlearn not listening.
ego will never get you as far as your heart.
you never know who looks up to you.
people remember how you treat them.
love matters most when times are roughest.
magic happens when you choose to love.
you don't have to take anyone's advice.

***

the fourteenth thing to always remember is you'll offend people while on your path. not intentionally. your choices to follow your purpose can make people who haven't followed theirs uncomfortable and they will tell you you're being foolish and unreasonable and should choose the road most comfortable)like them(.

how to not offend people. keep going. when you keep going you inspire those same people to one day do the same. to not get stuck on trying to please everyone. knowing a third of everyone you come in contact may softly or greatly disagree with you keeps more of your energy with you instead of trying to convince others. that is there work to do. yours is just to be you. willing to do the right thing as love leads you.

grow through what you are going through.

when you grow through what you are going through you always come out better. you always come back better.

possibilities to let in.

let in the possibility that you are ready.
for whatever happens. for whatever comes.

let in the possibility that you'll be fine.
take the leap. trust yourself.

let in the possibility that it's your time.
you'll never know if you don't try.

let in the possibility that you need to do this.
don't worry if it won't work out. you've gotten
this far and you haven't even used your wings.

***

sometimes you put yourself never. put yourself last. now is the time to put you on top. that is long overdue.

how to use your wings. i know the feeling of gliding the feeling of falling the feeling of rising above strong head winds. i also know when things get tough and you have to try and you have to flap and you have to go against so much but it feels like you are going nowhere. been there. but that is the practice. that is the way to see if what you are made of is made for that place for that person for that gives you so much information for you to consider if the air up there is your where. if you want to be there but may be too big there or too small there or just right there. think about where you are in life. are you in flight. are you on a perch. are you gliding. are you falling. are you soaring. are you seeking something. then determine the size of your wings needed for you to get there and strive there. thrive there. let in the possibility that your wings aren't done growing and your wingspan will reach further than you can imagine.

what you deserve to feel.

you deserve to feel more love.
you deserve to feel more light.
you deserve to feel more peace.
you deserve to feel more space.
you deserve to feel more balance.
you deserve to feel more grace.
you deserve to feel more support.
you deserve to feel more energy.
you deserve to feel more wonder.
you deserve to feel more you.
you deserve to feel more.
you deserve to feel.

***

you deserve to feel more you. boundless. balanced. blessed. bountiful. beautiful. brilliant. if you're around people that make you feel less then those are not your people.

the season of being taken advantage of has passed. no longer an option. they add value or they go away. there is no in-between.

how to find your people. everything isn't always in plain sight. as chance has it the best way to find your people is to go where you must step out of your comfort zone and into chance. into and through an archway that holds where you're supposed to go and you only know that if and when you pass the threshhold. sounds ridiculous or sounds basic but it is. that all you have to do is do something you normally wouldn't do or do what you typically do and be the threshhold for someone else. it isn't an either or. it is and and and. be a bridge and a bridge. you will always walk into your person your people along the path of chance and risk.

pay close attention

to how you feel around certain people.
to when you choose to go where you don't want to.
to lopsided relationships you always revive.
to lessons that come out of hardship.
to moments you are the happiest.

stay where you're supposed to be.
leave when you need to leave.
start listening to your heart
and breathe deeply
while letting go
of what others think.

***

how to pay attention. stay where you're supposed to stay. leave when you need to leave. start listening to your heart and breathe deeply while letting go of what others think. in that process there is a clearing an opening a glimpse into the next. the next window. the next treasure. the next love. the next chapter. to revive you to re-energize you to give you a second wind when the first just isn't cutting it if you've given up on it. on opening. on glimpsing. on trying. on loving. there is always hope there. always hope there. when you pinpoint exactly what you want. not every day will go your way and not every love will be the last. but there are clues in the gaps in the crevices in the energy you feel. energy is the oldest truth teller. such wisdom in vibes. such wisdom in intuition. patience yourself to notice yourself and get hella interested in the tide of you. the still of you. the depth of you. the shallow of you. and compass yourself with all your landmarks all your heartmarks and give yourself permission to see yourself as is. love yourself as is.

handle you with care.

handle you with care.

what to focus on

what you can control. your love. your time.
what is important. your truth. your heart.
what you need. your rest. your health.
what is yours. your respect. your worth.
what you deserve. your power. your freedom.

it's not about finding the right words.
it's about finding your feelings. finding
what is closest)as close as you can get(
to what needs to be acknowledged. and
anyone who sits with you stays with you
while you focus on you is the one for you.

how to focus on what you can control. become disinterested in stories that haven't played out. root yourself in what you know.

how to focus on what is important. reward yourself with little victories that you prioritize. do harder things before the easy things.

how to focus on what you need. be in constant conversation with what is necessary for you to function and thrive and require that.

how to focus on what is yours. latch on to the idea that you are no one's but yours. you are always yours. and trust in all that you do.

how to focus on what you deserve. lean on your boundaries and don't compromise your standards. onward with your heart's desire.

belonging is a love hope.

you belong everywhere you want to be.
you belong where your dreams take you.
you belong in better safer relationships.
you belong even if you feel like you don't.
you belong and should hold your head up.

if anyone if anyone does you wrong
plagues you with their own stuff their
own insecurities their own cage tell
them tell them no more. stand up
stand out stand away from that
drama. you always belong.

***

you belong to yourself. and your temple your crown your heart your light can't be dimmed even if they try. standing tall is for all those previous times you were made to feel small by people scared of your presence. my goodness your presence is the greatest presence.

how to find belonging. make a t-chart with three headers: seen. heard. loved. underneath each write all the people and places that it is true for you. write in where you want that to be true for you. that tells you where to leave and where to seek.

belonging is a love hope.
it says:

you belong. any where. every where. you are seen here.
you are loved here. you are needed here. you make it better
here. stay here. be here. you can be fully here. all you here.
you are deeply loved here. proud of you here.

no one like you.

no one gives like you. effortlessly.
no one loves like you. deeply.
no one glows like you. stunningly.
no one holds like you. thoughtfully.

can't be anyone but you. and having you
)even on days you feel like not being you
even on days far from feeling any good(
is the best person to have. the best one
to choose. the best one to rely. don't
get down and think you are done.
down is still the greatest you.

***

for choosing to be anyone but you takes you further away from you. who you're meant to be. who you're needing more. others look to others to see if some of them are for them. you look to others and remind them to be them. don't fall in the trap of being someone you're not.

how to choose you. wonder more about who you are. currently. don't judge you. don't ridicule you. don't blame you. just name you. all of you. as much of you as you know. and for each part of you you expressed wonder if there is one or more parts of you missing that you still need to bring up for air. these can be adjectives. these can be values. these can be identities. these can be whatever you like. this is you. this is for you. no one can make you do anything you don't want to. but part of you is acknowledging you. then wonder a bit more about how each part of you impacts the parts of others. are you a bridge or a barrier. keep the bridges. inventory your barriers. and choose to be the you that inspires others to do the same.

on leaving.

leaving is another type of bloom.
you become what you couldn't
by leaving places not ready
for your prowess.

***

for leaving is a journey. some leave in place. some leave in presence. some leave and you don't know they are elsewhere. however you leave)you're leaving now(shed shed shed what you don't need and keep keep keep what need be kept.

how to leave. think about when you drift. how often you drift. do you wander away from someone while they are with you. it is one of the dopest skills to be able to be tuned into someone completely the entire time they are sharing or spending time with them. but the mind is an interesting instrument that sometimes tells us it needs something else in order to concentrate or stay interested or find another thing. be aware of this. when you do this. how you do this. you already do this. leaving. up to you if you want to train your mind in another way or let it keep dictating to you what it needs you to do to find equilibrium.

if no matter what you do to be present isn't working. like bringing your attention back to them. not interrupting and making it about you. request a quick break to get water or a walk and come back refreshed. you may not be into them. you may not be into that. you may be forcing yourself to bloom in a space that won't allow your bloom. so then you must away expeditiously with caution for your beloved bloom to have everything it needs to bloom wildly as it was meant to be. some may say leaving is a form of failure but it is a form of finding what fits. it's okay to advocate for your bloom.

for when you just want to turn back.

when you have a lot on your mind. and your body tosses and turns. and you can feel all the tension occupy your soul. a breaking point is headed your way. you will want to turn back retreat into comfort. distance yourself from what's through the next door. the next page. the next chapter. but it is what you've been wanting for. waiting for. working for. yeah it would be preferred to know what's on the other side the way you've pictured it but life is a challenging journey. challenge yourself. dare yourself. to brave into a beautiful you.

***

right now it may feel heavy and unknown and trying and it is easier to revert back into habits into relationships into situations that are comfortable but toxic. or comfortable but exhausted. or comfortable and ending. believe in you. hope in you. breathe in you. and break into the next next with confidence knowing it will be what you need it to be once you get there. because you are there to get you there.

how to not turn back. whether this was just the next page you turned to or you searched in the index to find this as this moment speaks to you what you can do and what you should do is ask yourself what the lesson is right now. where is the lesson right now. is there something you need to learn right now. is there something you need to unlearn right now. what is most helpful right now is that you are aware that there is an imbalance and you are being proactive to to get to the root of it. so root to it. root for you.

four reminders to inhale twice.

when you put in work results come.
you are the answer you are looking for.
having high standards means you care.
standing up for yourself is a love hope.

when you put in work results come.
you are the answer you are looking for.
having high standards means you care.
standing up for yourself is a love hope.

bring these. take these. breathe these. say these.
you are all these and infinity more. carry on love.

how to stand up for you. standing. up right. forthright. as this is your right to stick up for you for all things you know to be good and true. some have been given the green light to not care for how they impact those around them and some had to navigate with lights always red. even if no one understands you aren't doing this for them or their validation. you are doing this for the future you.

standing up for you is a love hope.
it says:

this isn't my normal. putting myself out there. there were times it backfired and things became worse than before but it is vital to still speak truth to power speak truth to trauma speak truth to moments where the least resistant choice maintains the status quo but isn't what is best what is right what is important is i don't have all the answers but i have my experience my heart my question is why it's okay for you to speak up and be heard but when i speak up i'm told to sit down. no more. no more. this is my shield to roar. to roar. to roar.

never never too much too much.

one of the most interesting things
anyone could ever say is that you
are too much. too soft. too quiet.
too loud. too big. too bold. too
over the top. too fast. too slow.
too this. too that. too too too.
what you should hear is that you
are just too much beauty in one
person for them. too much love
is the best love. it overflows.
meaning you are always full
and spilling. full and spilling.

***

if too much should be language that leaves their lips to dictate you determine them out of touch out of line out of time. for too much from you is merely one thousandth of a percent of you they wish they had.

how to be too much. it's an art. being you. and like any piece of art there are interpretations not worth entertaining or explaining. there is no need for you to entertain or explain you to anyone you don't want to or feel safe to. too much for anyone is their problem.

twelve pressures to let go of.

the pressure to get it all done.
the pressure to be perfect.
the pressure to finish strong.
the pressure to know what to do.
the pressure to fit in a box.
the pressure to be productive.
the pressure to shed your culture.
the pressure to remain the same.
the pressure to backburn your dreams.
the pressure to keep your feelings in.
the pressure to heal quickly.
the pressure to respond.

***

diamonds are created under the right conditions of heat and pressure. and there are just some who can't stand to be around the temperature of you. you are already formed but polishing keeps you shining. and sometimes it is your shine that some want to latch on so they benefit from your light. but if the pressure isn't yours and it is coming elsewhere that you deem unnecessary and unhealthy you should make the best move for you.

how to let go of pressure. when you let go of all that pressure that isn't yours you feel better. you fill better. and let in what nourishes you instead of what hurts you. all pressure ain't good pressure. always ask yourself where is this coming from what can i control and do i have to do this or else you'll always carry what isn't yours to hold.

four things we all have in common.

we're all healing from something.
we're all learning from something.
we're all breaking from something.
we're all growing from something.

for just a moment zoom out. further out. beyond yourself. and pan above above. you might assume those you know are fine. strangers are fine. their people are fine. but everyone isn't fine. it can seem that way. from the outside. this need to show up as fine is what is harming us. we're just getting better at hiding it. you aren't alone. we all deserve grace.

***

you are kind in that you kind. in that you care. in that your only expectation for others is that anything from them is steeped in love.

how to give grace to others. know that they are human. that they cannot be perfect. that they can only stand on water on concrete and not on the ocean. to ask how's their heart not just if things are feeling off but as a normal check in question so you establish a relationship that is genuine and not transactional. transactional relationships are only as good as the input. and most times that input has everything but love. you give others grace by listening and letting them know directly you are there if they need so when they need you or are dealing with something they can be honest instead of having to greet you in their mask to play pretend to fake to distance to shut off that part of them they should be able to bring with them to every space they decorate with their existence.

this one is to remind you to smile.

just want to let you know
that you will always always
be their best. their best love.
their best first. their best one.
their best friend. their best best.
their best that made them feel
like they were the only.
the only in the room. the only
one that matters. the only one
who goes to the deep end and
goes deeper. deeper. you are so
cherished. so damn cherished.

***

when you realize how beautiful a giver you are you'll have done a thousand more beautiful things. a thousand more selfless things. a thousand more loving things. and still won't know what i'm talking about. you're so so cherished. so damn cherished.

how to be their best. by being you. yes that sounds like what you already heard but you're hands down the best anyone has come across because you don't try so hard to go out of your way being anyone but you. the best treatment is you. your big heart. your tendency to be a giver when your someone feels like they don't deserve your world class treatment. being their best means being your best. not in that you overtry overextend overexert overlove you just go out and do your daily. your bestly is by far the best love they have ever experienced because you don't try to fix them. that isn't your station that isn't your call that isn't your mission. you can't see it but you are what prayers consist of. you are the best blessing.

12 love lessons.

can't hide from yourself any longer.
what's meant for you is yours if you want it bad enough.
everything is a practice. consistency will alter your life.
faith plus action plus trust are necessary ingredients for success.
collective trauma means everyone is trying to figure out how to heal the best they know how.
you have to process the little stuff before they become bigger.
vulnerability cleanses you.
love flourishes you.
culturally competent therapy is transformative.
you have to bet on yourself.
to make waves you must get in the water and
believe you can stand on your own.

***

you already knew this. you just didn't have the language to explain this. explain you. but you found you by looking for you. more to uncover but there is no shame in loving you by watering your own roots.

how to water your own roots. ground yourself. either sitting down or standing up. if standing find something natural like a tree or long sturdy walking stick and plant yourself firmly as nature anchors you up. feel the energy of it extend its gift to you while you close your eyes and focus on the internal dialogue it is having with you. if you are sitting find your grounding with what you are sitting on as if that is your core. breathe in and out. in and out. tell yourself what you need to hear. say nothing. move nothing. let your mind travel where it wants then bring it back to your breath. take the shape of what is anchoring or grounding you and imagine this practice as one way to spend time with you and your roots. do this right now.

the ones for you do these four things consistently.

when they ask about your mental health.
when they remind you to take a breath.
when they say you deserve rest.
when they attentively listen.

this is how you know who to stay close to.
this is how you know who has learned your
heart language. this is how you know who
has all the parts of you in heart. this is what
it is like to be heard. when they don't just
speak the words but show you why you
chose them. you know who to keep.
you know who to let go.

***

not just anyone can access you. call it a privilege. call it a right. call it whatever you like. but make sure you protect your heart.

how to protect your heart. you know all of the questions that need to be asked. ask them. you know everything that you deserve. demand them. you know when the energy is off. don't chase off energy. keep it direct. this doesn't mean be mean or jagged or intense it just means you require clarity and what the plan is what the intention is where this is headed before you make any next moves. it is the mature thing to do. to wonder out loud and communicate sincerely. to check to see if this is the page you want to be on and if this is the rest stop you want your heart connected to. stop responding to what never responds to you. just because the idea of something sounds nice doesn't mean the reality of it belongs in your life. because when you are unlocked there isn't a valve to stop you from giving you. it will be their honor to protect your heart, too.

you don't need

extravagant love.
shallow love.
half love.

you need

profound love.
consistent love.
omnipresent love.

stop apologizing
for what you need.

***

when you stand by your needs they manifest. watch who stays. don't run after who leaves.

how to weed out what you don't need. notice how you feel when certain people and energies are around you. notice how you feel when certain people and energies aren't around you. adjust the frequency and touch points and identify what helps you heal and what helps you hurt. make a plan to transition out all that cause damage effective immediately. that name that just popped up should be the first.

what you need to hear but haven't heard.

you've done enough. more than enough.
so much enough in the best enough kind
of way. no one does it like you. no one
can ever take your place. the lightest
from you is the brightest of you.
how do you do that. how do you do
you. how do you be you. how do you
make being you look so beautiful. don't
go. stay longer. here isn't the same without
you. a miracle to witness. the dopest heart
to kick it with. should have loved you
harder. will love you harder from now on.

***

a simple how are you gives you space to speak what needs to be spoken especially if the question comes from a lover a giver a kind kind soul truly interested in your wellbeing your heartbeing your wholebeing.

how to say how are you in a language they understand. with care. with consideration. some people just don't have a lot of free time to share everything they have going on. but you can send a message with zero pressure for them to return it. you can say you don't want anything except for them to know you're thinking of them. that if they ever have a chance to come up for air they know you are there to breathe with them)you're breathing wiith them now(. feels good to know your people don't put pressure on the limited water you have.

love hopes for you.

i hope someone loves you the way you love.
not just the feel good kind. but the deep good
kind. the bottomless kind. the longest kind.

i hope the day deserves you. comforts you.
reaches you without needing to ask it to.
warms you. fills you. guides you home.

i hope you follow what needs to be followed
and get away from what needs to be released.

i hope you know how loved you are. that your
person your people your community wraps their
love around you to remind you so that you know
so that you know so that you know that you are
loved down to your bones and beyond.

i hope you win back what may have been a loss.
that you get returned what was taken and reclaim
it as a lesson to do even better because now you
are better. you've always been better.

i hope you cross your own mind. cross your own
heart. cross your own being. and center yourself.
honor yourself. appreciate yourself. as an act off
self love. as an act of self revolution. self healing.

i hope whatever you hide inside from the outside
know that it's okay to be you. that you are able to
fully accept you as you.

love hopes for you. II

i hope you understand how the magnitude of you
really is such a significant gift. beautiful treasure.
the depth of you is such a sight to see.

love hopes for you. III

i hope someone breathes you in not to just breathe
you out. and that they draw you in the clouds and
replay how you spoke your name for the first
time so they remember what it was like not
to be able to catch their breath. that they
look at you as if memorizing every
curve every dimple every mark
every every every so they can
specifically tell the story
of you. i hope i hope
someone deserves
your beauty.

truths about you.

being around you feels like a holiness. a sacred peace that shouldn't be taken advantage of.

you are pure poetry. undefined. complex with hidden messages. beautiful meanings. a slow prayer not just anyone can breathe.

people see you. but only the chosen few can feel you. understand you. grasp you. get close enough to ever say they've been touched by an angelic soul.

you are worth fighting for. rolling up your heart dropping the ego and loving stronger for.

everyone's favorite giver. you know what someone needs before they know they need it. evergiving. evergiving. a gorgeous humangiving.

love pours from the depths of you. the deepest of you. no matter how hard you try to pour from shallow waters there is nothing there because there is nothing shallow about you.

your love hope is you.

just because you won't settle for anything less than what you deserve doesn't make you harsh. it makes you healthy because you respect you enough to not accept subpar relationships. when you find someone who shows you more. takes you back to you and helps revive you and parts of you others told you weren't beautiful. they remind you of your lost language. and)keyword and(. don't expect anything in return except being you so they can be them. that is magic love.

so much beauty in you. so much light in you.
so much good in you. so much you in you.
by embracing who you are you respond
to what your heart really wants. what
your soul really needs. and that is
choosing to be you. being you.
your love hope is you.

***

how to speak your language. if they don't catch on to your light and what makes you light and what brings you joy then their attention isn't the attention you need. no matter how much you think it will feel good it won't fill good and will end as quickly as it began. to speak your language there has to be earnesty and honesty to not try to change you into someone that isn't you. to mold you into a voice that mutes you. to iron you into a place that doesn't fit you. there must be determination to let you be and in that being you can be seen and heard and appreciated the way you make them feel seen and heard and appreciated. that's that love. that kind of love that doesn't teach it explores and mirrors and opens and unlocks and observes with curiosity with no desire to control your wild heart.

how to)re(discover love.

spill into someone. without looking for credit. without wondering if they will return it. without looking ahead at if they say how special you made them feel. take you out of it and focus focus focus on them.

convert all the words all the words you sing sweetly to others and inject them swiftly into you. cover you in deep affirmations. smother you in honey and radiate the vibes you want in and evict the vibes you want out.

no more searching for validation in the same place that denies you the validation you deserve.

gift wrap your heart. how you like it wrapped. tight enough. soft enough. loved enough. and always open you and surprise you. because you are the best package. the best person. the best anyone could ever get. the best love anyone could ever get.

you are the best love anyone could ever get.

you are the best love anyone could ever get.
you are the best love anyone could ever get.
you are the best love anyone could ever get.
you are the best love anyone could ever get.
you are the best love anyone could ever get.
you are the best love anyone could ever get.
you are the best love anyone could ever get.
you are the best love anyone could ever get.
you are the best love anyone could ever get.
you are the best love anyone could ever get.
you are the best love anyone could ever get.
you are the best love anyone could ever get.
you are the best love anyone could ever get.
you are the best love anyone could ever get.
you are the best love anyone could ever get.
you are the best love anyone could ever get.
you are the best love anyone could ever get.
you are the best love anyone could ever get.
you are the best love anyone could ever get.
you are the best love anyone could ever get.
you are the best love anyone could ever get.
you are the best love anyone could ever get.
you are the best love anyone could ever get.
you are the best love anyone could ever get.
you are the best love anyone could ever get.
you are the best love anyone could ever get.
you are the best love anyone could ever get.
you are the best love anyone could ever get.
you are the best love anyone could ever get.
you are the best love anyone could ever get.
you are the best love anyone could ever get.
you are the best love anyone could ever get.

how to)re(discover love. II

go back to your last heartache. when you felt
most tender. and didn't think you would feel
better. and didn't think you'd get over them.
and didn't think your would would ever tilt
like it used to tilt. now touch your body where
your heart beats skin. feel that. feel that.
what once was everything has gotten
you to now. and here you are. here.
here. breathing. promising to be.
promising to)re(discover love
that never left. never left.

you always love again.

i don't want to spoil the ending.
but you love again.
you always love again.

necessary reminders.

you are in a league of your own. many emulate
you but they cannot be you. don't drain you.
inspiration from you is like water in a desert.

chasing your dream doesn't mean others
can't chase theirs. there is so much room
for everyone to beam. don't hoard the
light. don't hoard the light.

the effort you put in won't always bear fruit
as fast as you want it to. results may take time
be delayed but know)truly know(the yield
is coming. it's always coming.

your love can't be measured or evaluated.
people will always have something to say.
at the end of the day your love matters
most when you know you tried you
gave your all you accounted for
what wasn't your best and in
your heart you know that
your love your love
lives in places
people can't
always
see.

how to see your love. if they have to ask they aren't ready for you.

what abundance finds.

abundance finds those who manifest.
abundance finds those who attract.
abundance finds those who believe.
abundance finds those who act.

***

how to manifest. set reasonable intentions.

how to attract. have your intentions always in mind.

how to believe. with burning passion knowing it is yours to claim.

how to act. dedicated in pursuit without letting the fire burn out.

healing words.

someone loses sleep over you. thinking of you.
pacing and hoping you carry them in your heart
too. they are content made whole knowing you
exist. don't think for one more minute no one
cares about you. that no one cries about you.
you just visited them again. on their mind
on their wavelengh right now right now.
your energy is a necessary healing that
everyone needs more of. and your
person your person who holds
you in high esteem needs
you to read this.

waves of you.

there are layers of you unlayered. undiscovered.
unweathered. unearthing. under more water. and
knowing that you already already are in bloom.
already already outgrowing where you are.
already all ready to move on. into more.
into new. into you. the waves of you.
is beautiful proof that whatever
happens you will unfold and
find deeper parts of you.
versions of you. that
have waited to fill
you. to love you.

***

your waves are breathgiving. the crash. the pull. the gather. the gather. nothing like it. nothing like you. no one like you. may you love the waves of you. the depths of you. and ocean how you ocean. without hesitation. without worry. without question. wave on. wave on.

how to find deeper parts of you. cherish the great unlearn. the great ability to find more of what is there not to perfect but to aware. not to condemn but to hold. not to arrest but to seek. there is always more of you more for you. no need to announce you or broadcast you or put you on a pedestal. this is for you to keep watering you)remember one way to water your roots this here is another(to trip you to take you to tell you that every part of you is the companion your favorite person admires about you. travel towards you and say to you *look what i found i love you i appreciate you i see you i honor you i admire you i cherish you i thank you i accept you i accept you i accept you i accept you i accept you i accept you i accept you.*

five ways to maintain meaningful connection.

display kindness.
recite kindness.
give kindness.
affirm kindness.
become kindness.

everyone is going through something.
practicing kindness goes a long long way.
you never know who needs it. you never
know how one small act inspires others
to do the same. pay kindness forward.
become the kindness that you seek.

***

when you become kindness you inspire others to do the same. they pay it forward and everyone feels loving light.

how to kind when you don't feel like being kind. imagine on your worst day someone extends to you an unnecessary hardship an unecessary blockage an unecessary response that could have been avoided but instead makes your day even worse. that person didn't know you were having a bad day but you know they were having a bad day and it wasn't about you. but instead of giving back to them the words that acts the response they responded to you and you returned to them a smile and an are you okay and an i hope you have a better day and go on about your day that may seem too much load on you to re-direct because you have every right to say something unkind or do something unkind to top their unkindness but imagine for a moment that each person takes a breath before doing anything and wonders if the next thing they do beautifully benefits positively someone else. kindness is contagious. spread it.

what intimacy looks like.

you. the way you up.
you. the way you arrive.
you. the way you reflect.
you. the way you ignite.

how to be intimate. it can't always be about you. you have to hold back making it about you. you have to lean into every word every breath every sigh between sighs and annotate what they are saying without saying. and then when they feel like they are complete)ask if they are complete(they tend on you. they tend on you. they give you the attention you gifted them.

this.

a grip. a connection. a pulse
isn't about fixing. it is about showing.
showing up. showing care. showing love.
showing activity. actively. acting. doing
something that isn't self serving. this.
intimacy. is an ongoing dance. a
lyric and a hum. a two-part
harmony. a present.
a presence.

thank you.

thank you. you don't hear this enough.
thank you. for everything. literally. every thing.
thank you. for carrying all the emotional burdens.
thank you. for absorbing all the emotional labor.
thank you. for surviving all the emotional burdens.
thank you. for holding all the emotional labor.

but you shouldn't have to. you deserve a break.
not just a momentary rest and then grit it back.
a clean break. a weight lifted off your shoulders.
for someone else to take the torch. for someone
else to think about all the things you have to
think about. all the things you have to hold.
for someone else to cover what you cover.
because it is a lot to juggle and not drop.
a lot to still stand when it feels there
is nothing under you to stand on.

thank you. for standing.
thank you. for centering.
thank you. for rocking.
thank you. for healing.
thank you. for alling.
thank you. for being.

***

strong hasn't seen your kind of beautiful strength.

how to say thank you. daily. this momently. for doing what you are supposed to do can be thankless. heartless. so take this embed this share this exactly partially in your own words to you to someone.

because of you.

you are loved because you are you.
that may feel strange or overstated.
or you've heard every line before.
but you shake so many hearts
without even trying.

while others try to be like others you stay you. and that mirror)that mirror(ever soul looks at in you is the most profound reflection. the most profound reflection. because of you they are willing)so willing(to uproot themselves to find better soil. better situations. better predicaments. better better. better better.

and while it is easy to take on the drama. take on the gossip. take on the negativity. you. you. you. have this power about you to redirect and breathe to diffuse. breathe reminders to focus on what is important. but you are human mixed with moon. and the water in you emotions. pulls in what others feel and you personally turn their stuff into yours love.

how to find better soil. talking about people shows us that we are social beings. that we need each other. but that doesn't mean we have to harm one another. if the culture is to bash and put down instead of elevate and support that environment you're in is toxic. hard to grow where you can't be and breathe. you can be the one that stirs love in the system to create the change everyone deserves or you follow that buzzing in your heart and find new air new soil to blossom in. remember: leaving is a form of finding what fits. not to blend in and be like the others and lose your sense of self but being able to become your full expression without having to defend or guard or fortify or hide so others can be and you cannot. so start digging. detecting. wandering. so much is out there for you. waiting for you. you'll know you're in better soil almost instantly.

because of you. II

and because of that)because of you(
that lover that giver that wonder that
unbelievable heart doesn't need more.
more stress. more strain. more that
isn't yours. but because you are you
you will try to solve and fix and pour
your energy where it isn't always
appreciated. where they take you
for granted. no more. no more.

it's okay to remove yourself.
and replant yourself. because
you)because of you(are the
last most beautiful love
no just anyone
can access.

***

how to replant yourself. trustingly. taking with you all of you knowing you will land where you land and be okay in your landing. it will feel awkward and unclear and unstable and unknown and under no pretense should you question the replant process)it's normal if you question the replant process(as one that you shouldn't have done and you should have stayed where you were but if you stay where you are you just end up filling the same inhaling the same and there is a reason you have to get away have to be away have to go where you are celebrated and and and that is part of the process. to question. to scrutinize. to settle. but if you want to take a chance dare yourself to do what is uncomfortable for the sake of becoming comfortable. for the sake of fully living not just going through the motions. you deserve better love. you deserve better.

consistency you deserve.

consistent love.
consistent friendship.
consistent trust.
consistent peace.
consistent energy.

fall in love with the kind of people
who are consistent. those that don't
ghost you then return as if nothing
happened. align yourself with love
that doesn't have to be questioned.
love that loves you back.

***

you are a constant constant. an always there kind of love. you pour. you spill. you give. inspiring others to be constants too.

how to be consistent. acknowledge that being consistent is challenging. to be able to be and do what has been and done day in and day out. can be exhausting. can be too high a standard to exist in. but consistency doesn't mean perfectly. consistency means heartly. consistency means intentionally. consistency means willingly. to be open to each day and try. to slowly transition one word to the next word one line to the next line one page to the next page one chapter after the next chapter one book after the next book. in your fashion. in your tenor. in your pace. to decipher between being someone you can be proud of and who others you love and care for can come to or speak to or reach to for goodness because what you grow you are. so if you grow love you are love. if you grow hate you are hate. so be love. be. love. grow. love. consistently. we need more love. we need more of you love. choose to be love. choose to be love.

if anything you are yours. always yours.

some will claim you are hard to contact. hard to connect. hard to reach. you are. but they say that is if it were bad. as if you are inclined to give energy freely to anyone just because. but tell that to your heart. tell that to your scars. tell that to wounds still tender still open still learning to heal. you have every right)every goddamn right(to withhold. to contain. to reserve you. make no justification. no excuse. no reason. to explain why you keep you to you. if anything you are yours. always yours. and can decide your moves your decisions your indecisions your reasons your whys your nothings your alls. the greatest feeling is a liberated soul. one that no one can define but you. for you. by you. how you want to. why to. when to. where to. what to. such peace. when each piece of you is loved.

***

each piece of you is loved. each piece of you is loved.
each piece of you is loved. each piece of you is loved.
each piece of you is loved. each piece of you is loved.
each piece of you is loved. each piece of you is loved.
each piece of you is loved. each piece of you is loved.
each piece of you is loved. each piece of you is loved.
each piece of you is loved. each piece of you is loved.
each piece of you is loved. each piece of you is loved.
each piece of you is loved. each piece of you is loved.
each piece of you is loved. each piece of you is loved.
each piece of you is loved. each piece of you is loved.
each piece of you is loved. each piece of you is loved.
each piece of you is loved. each piece of you is loved.
each piece of you is loved. each piece of you is loved.
each piece of you is loved. each piece of you is loved.
each piece of you is loved. each piece of you is loved.
each piece of you is loved. each piece of you is loved.

turn your sails towards yourself and keep sailing.

the person you disappoint the most will be you if you keep letting others tell you what you should do and who you should love.

the person you disappoint the most will be you if you keep investing your heart in people in places who invest nothing in you.

the person you disappoint most will be you if you keep thinking things will change by staying in toxic relationships that don't care.

the person you disappoint most will be you if you keep pouring your beautiful gifts talents treasures where your heart doesn't want to be.

the person you disappoint the most will be you if you keep wading in waters established just to take what they can from you and then leave you capsized and stranded fending for yourself. but what those people don't know about you is that no matter the situation you survive. you just add more water. more light. more conviction. more lessons. more appreciation. for understanding you are just closer to what is meant for you. all things won't work out and that is fine. don't close yourself off. turn your sails towards yourself and keep sailing.

***

how to sail towards yourself and keep sailing. as this is at the end know that this is really the beginning. a preview. a trailer. before the curtain is pulled and you see what is really behind it. for now these are all just words. just nudges. just flag posts. just bits of a whole. and the only way to sail towards you and keep sailing is actively using these pages as a working document. as a working you. as a tool to retool and resharpen your already overflowing toolbox. reading this is a start in your direction. keep going then go back.

you get to decide.

you get to decide what you water.
you get to decide who you water.
you get to decide where you water.
you get to decide how you water.

when they want to come back.

ask them why they left. with your absence.
ask them why they stopped. with your silence.
ask them why they forgot. with your boundaries.
ask them why they lied. with your closure.

to them you may have been a little heart.
a someone before the next someone. a stop
before their final destination. how foolish.
how small. how unknowing. how careless.
how their loss will rock them for the rest
of their rest. let that be their end. let this
not deter you. you are on to far greater.

***

someone's forever. always. their first true memory of love. and to the others an almost. a someone they let slip away when their heart was too small to let your brilliance in.

you deserve a love that tries its hardest to keep you. not a love that tries to deprive you and take you further away from who you're meant to bloom into.

how to respond when they want to come back. with a blinking cursor. or left on read. or left unread. or with a flat out no. or with what is noted up above. whatever you do don't feel bad for doing it. there comes a time when you can't anymore. the warn is the once. the deed then done. and there is no coming around after that if that is how you operate. whether in absence or silence or boundaries or closure this is your guidebook for each version of you that you hue into that you mature into after sun fades into each day. the great thing is that you are the forecast and you create your own weather.

if no one has told you yet.

you are worth staying up late vibing to.
you belong they just don't deserve your presence.
someone is reciting your name over their heart.
someone is breathing your energy thinking of you.
mirrors look to you for guidance. for approval.
for validation. and you say just be. and that is
by far the most beautiful permission.
you speak the language of souls. straight to
the heart. straight to the core. deep healing
happens around whoever you are near.
saying no is a form of necessary self care.
in the moment you might feel pressured to not
want to let them down while letting you down.
say yes to you more by practicing saying no
to what you don't want to do. let you up.
they will be okay. you have an infinite amount
of grace to give yourself. use it. anoint it. rub it
on your heart. you have every right to take
the love you need and give it to yourself
anytime. any time.

how to tell yourself what you need to hear. it can feel off-putting to have to tell you what you need to hear if you don't know what you need to hear. but you know. like right now there is a stirring in you wondering what it would be like if someone just said that thing even if you don't want to admit it would be nice to hear that thing. complimenting. seeing. appreciating. adorning. so in that absence of a someone either publically or privately you can place messages on your windows on your computer screen on your laptop near the keyboard with brevity or symbol or direct quotes that lift your heart even if you change the name of an alarm and you wake up to your own affirmation do that. do that. no shame in raising your crown.

i statements you deserve to feel.

i appreciate you. how you show up and change any mood. the way you center and balance and caress and smile with your heart. **i honor you**. for still being you still loving you still standing you against all the odds all the difficult all the issues that have stormed your soul. **i love you**. the you not everyone experiences or takes time to get to know. **i hear you**. your feelings are yours and valid. tell me more. **i see you**. whole you. complete you. the figuring it out you. **i want you**. to feel how you make others feel. you are absolutely amazing. absolutely amazing.

***

the most deserving are those that second themselves. last themselves. as they are considered to be front line givers. front line lovers. for they are willing to sacrifice so others may reap benefits of the light they divert from them so that more can grow. and in that fronting there is a forgetting that happens. a forgetting that keeps score in the soul. a thankless forgetting that must be abolished from the hearts of those that gain advantage without knowing they have an advantage. not saying you should strike in order for there to be better knowing on their behalf)you most definitely can strike(just saying someone should be your front, too. someone should be by your side, too. someone should have your back, too. someone should hold your love, too.

how to say i statements without them coming off empty. you learn your person. deeply. with a craving to lift even the slightest burden they could carry but you graciously take off their shoulders. just by observation. just by paying loving attention and asking questions that you know the answer to but the asking is beautiful consideration they thought you'd never care to ask. action. not words. do the words without hesitation. let your love testify out loud.

your love is

giving. always about others.
sacred. to be treated as such.
affectionate. fluent in love.
unselfish. beautifully kind.
soft. healing and powerful.

your love isn't

to be taken for granted or contained. isolated
or made to feel belittled. your love isn't fragile.
and isn't for those unready for challenge. truth.
growth. passion. your love is the highest honor.

***

your love. the highest honor.
your love. the deepest depth.
your love. the rarest rare.
your love. the greatest gift.
beholding you is one wish
every soul wishes for.

how to stay sacred. sacredness is an internal craft. an internal flame. an internal alchemy. it is within you to elevate you. to only do the opposite of lowering. highering you is valuing you so you can attract what you brew and make no allowances for anything other than sacred relationships.

what doesn't exist

a perfect person.
a perfect relationship.
a perfect job.
a perfect solution.
a perfect life.

what does exist

your ability to be despite the pressure to perfect.
the best part about you is that nothing is perfect.
somehow love from you feels like perfect love.
somehow love from you is the perfect dream.

***

how to love. you can't control anything or anyone but you. and there are times you can't even control you no matter what you do. but you can always infuse love. you can always radiate love. you can always think love. no matter the impact. no matter the result. no matter the yield. if it is done with good and kind and heart and hope and wellbeing then that is love. but you cannot pick and choose when and where you do that. that is too easy. to faucet. to reserve. to hoard. to keep away. the challenge will be to love in every step to love in every breath to love in situations you want to brim over with the opposite. and it can take everything out of you to take the road others aren't taking. but everything and in every thing there is a lesson. a love lesson. so if you fall from love next time bring a bit more with you. so instead of doing the first thing that comes to mind take a minute and pause and wonder what is being asked of. being required of you. and if you don't have the energy to come to it with love then wait until you can or just leave it in peace. no reason to not lead with love. hard to do but worth it love.

love hopes that fill you.

consistency.
reliability.
chemistry.
raw. real.
current.

a love that is earned through patience. no rushing. nothing good comes from rushing. don't want to miss any details of you.

consideration first.
wondering first.
heart first.

crashing into you. a precious colliding not to take lightly.
your lightly starts deeply. and if they can't wade they won't survive.

not keeping score of who gave what or who paid the way. the only thing to keep track is the feeling. that love)that kind of love(never keeps score. it just waves around on the waves of each other and meets each lover where they are and gives them the love they need. freedom. oh freedom. to be. to breathe. to travel. to move. to mistake. to discover. to dream. to unlearn. to fly and fall. to fly and fall. oh love. a love like that. a love like that. a asking. a curiosity. a dance. being there. not fixing. room to get close. not far enough to be far. holding space to shed. to grow. to share. to vulnerable. to listen.

how you know love hopes for you. anything from you is laced with love. and you deserve only love. the best love. not in idea but in execution. in every way. all ways. always. love needs you to exist for without you love is nothing. love is nothing. love is nothing. it longs and stays up thinking of you wanting you to want it too.

five hopes for you.
before you close this volume take five more with you.

protect your heart. from undeserving people and places.

do something. whatever point and place you are in this life you have the ability to make change. to see the gaps and needs of the world beyond yourself. care to do one small thing and that ripple will do monumental things.

re-commit to yourself. make this be a contract with you. to encourage you. to nudge you. to inspire you. to lean into spaces and practices that either are new to you or have collected dust. you are yours to do as you will and you deserve every chance to embrace you.

feel the love. no matter where you are or how you are or why you are you are enough. if you ever question if what you are doing is being seen or heard or valued or important it is you are you are. it is normal to not think that sometimes but know this all times.

hope for you. to become the best version of your beautiful self.

you have this book for a reason. a gift to you. a gift from someone. no matter how these words got to you they found you. they found you. now find you. go back to a page you couldn't see or didn't want to see or didn't find relevant and spend some time there. there is no rush here. this is no ordinary collection. this is for you to distribute you back to you. only you can do that. only you can enact that. just know that there is no judgment here. only love here. you are loved here.

xo. adrian michael
text me - 303.529.2197
for words you didn't know   **i appreciate you**
you needed to hear.

Made in the USA
Columbia, SC
09 September 2021